The
Money Magnet
Mindset

The

Money Magnet
Mindset

Tools to Keep You and Your Money on Track

Marie-Claire Carlyle

HAY HOUSE

Australia • Canada • Hong Kong • India
South Africa • United Kingdom • United States

First published and distributed in the United Kingdom by:
Hay House UK Ltd, 292B Kensal Rd, London W10 5BE.
Tel.: (44) 20 8962 1230; Fax: (44) 20 8962 1239.
www.hayhouse.co.uk

Published and distributed in the United States of America by:
Hay House, Inc., PO Box 5100, Carlsbad, CA 92018-5100.
Tel.: (1) 760 431 7695 or (800) 654 5126; Fax: (1) 760 431 6948 or (800) 650 5115.
www.hayhouse.com

Published and distributed in Australia by:
Hay House Australia Ltd, 18/36 Ralph St, Alexandria NSW 2015.
Tel.: (61) 2 9669 4299; Fax: (61) 2 9669 4144.
www.hayhouse.com.au

Published and distributed in the Republic of South Africa by:
Hay House SA (Pty), Ltd, PO Box 990, Witkoppen 2068.
Tel./Fax: (27) 11 467 8904. www.hayhouse.co.za

Published and distributed in India by:
Hay House Publishers India, Muskaan Complex, Plot No.3, B-2,
Vasant Kunj, New Delhi – 110 070. Tel.: (91) 11 4176 1620; Fax: (91) 11 4176 1630.
www.hayhouse.co.in

Distributed in Canada by:
Raincoast, 9050 Shaughnessy St, Vancouver, BC V6P 6E5.
Tel.: (1) 604 323 7100; Fax: (1) 604 323 2600

A catalogue record for this book is available from the British Library.

ISBN: 978-1-84850-844-6

Printed and bound in Great Britain by TJ International, Padstow, Cornwall.

Contents

Foreword

I was thrilled to be asked to write a foreword for Marie-Claire's new book, *Money Magnet Mindset*.

Creativity can make life exciting. The music that sends a chill down your spine, the painting that takes your breath away − both are a part of what creativity can do. Marie-Claire and her Money Magnet philosophy are routed in the importance of such creativity, the 'out-of-the-box thinking' that encourages innovation and making the commitment to break away from the same thought patterns that hold us back.

Marie-Claire magically captures the elixir of life, explaining the mindset you need to allow money to flow your way. Inspiring words about the law of magnetism − what we think about, we bring about − is one of her key messages. To succeed in life you need a happy and healthy mindset and this book will give you the practical tools to make this happen for you.

So enjoy this book: it will enlighten your thinking about money, develop your mindset to put you in the flow and help you become a real Money Magnet. But more than that, making money is a magical gift that can be used to help others, just as I did when I became a multimillionaire. In sharing my riches with people in need, I became more fulfilled and content myself.

Dr Dawn Gibbins MBE
Secret Millionaire and Philanthropist

Introduction

*'The only limitation is that which one
sets up in one's own mind.'*
– Napoleon Hill

There is one *essential* ingredient for attracting more money into your life – no matter how hard you work, if your *mind* isn't open to receiving more money, you will always stay at the same level of income.

If you accidentally attract more than your mind's 'allowance' – by, say, getting a pay rise or winning on the lottery – your mind will find a way to lose the money as quickly as possible. You might find that you have an unforeseen home repair that needs doing, for example, or you might decide to reward yourself with an extravagant holiday, or to help out a family friend who is in financial trouble. Your mind's job is to keep you safe, and to bring you back to the money level where it considers you *are* safe.

If this sounds a little crazy, take a look around you. You'll find that most people stay around the same level of income for most of their lives. You'll see lottery millionaires squander their money in no time at all because it doesn't feel safe to them to have so much of it all of a sudden. They don't know what to do with it, or who to trust for advice.

Take a look at your own pattern with money. How much do you have remaining at the end of each month or year? You may earn a lot of money, but if you are spending just as much as you earn, then your level is set extremely low. Recently, I heard about a stockbroker who spends £100,000 each week just on entertainment. This is someone who is earning a lot of money but who cannot accept and retain its full value.

Many people chase high earnings to prove they are 'good enough'. The trouble is, if underneath all the wealth achieved you still don't feel good enough, you will lose it just as quickly. I know, because it happened to me. I was driven by an urge to earn a high income so people would love and respect me. The problem was, I didn't love and respect myself, and as long as I didn't love and respect myself I spent my money irresponsibly.

> *'What you do with what you have is more important than what you have.'*
> – **Jim Rohn**

These beliefs are usually unconscious. I'm sure that stockbroker isn't purposefully throwing his money around in nightclubs to get people to like him. And I wasn't intentionally buying expensive toys and paintings just to be loved. No, this is what happens in the recesses of our unconscious minds – until we become conscious of it, of course!

My Story

My parents were entrepreneurs, so I knew how important it was to earn money. My focus was to earn lots of money, and so I went into sales. I learnt that I was particularly good at sales management, and soon I was responsible for £1million sales revenue every month as sales director of a UK software company.

Although I was earning a very generous six-figure salary, I was also spending just as much on entertainment, paintings and the occasional property. The amount I earned made little difference to the amount that was left in my pocket at the end of each month.

At the height of my success, I realized I was unhappy. My quest to be loved through earning lots of money had failed; I *still* felt unloved. My response was to leave my job and lose all the money I had accumulated. My unconscious reasoning was this: if having money didn't make me loved, maybe having *no* money would work. In fact, it did to a certain extent. I felt loved and cared for when I had no money. I felt incredibly supported, often by people who hadn't much money themselves. It was when I started to listen to people *with* money, though, that I realized something was wrong with the way I'd chosen to live my life. I looked at my reality and I saw that I was broke and in debt, and that I didn't love myself very much.

The first step was to start loving myself. Bit by bit, I learnt how to do this. I worked with mentors and buddies; I read uplifting books; I gave up looking for love elsewhere and chose to accept the love that had been inside of me all along. Then I looked to see what value I could offer to the world and I created the one-day Money Magnet Workshop. My book *How to Become a Money Magnet* followed, and that led to me helping more and more people to accept and love themselves, and in so doing, to attract more money for themselves... because they are worth it!

Before long, I was back to earning six figures, but this time I was doing what I loved, and enjoying the freedom that comes with running your own business.

Adopting a Money Magnet Mindset

This book is about training you to love and accept your full value in this world so you can also accept your full value in monetary terms. After all, money is the measure we use in our society. How do you know if you have been successful in business? You know by how many people you have helped, and by how much they are willing to give you in exchange for your help. Money is an accurate and helpful measure. It highlights what is really going on in your life, and if you are finding yourself short of money at the end of each month, there is something that needs addressing in how much you currently value yourself and your unique gifts.

Of course, you may not be aware of your unconscious beliefs about yourself or money. You are probably more conscious right now of the need to do something about your personal financial situation! In fact, that's probably why you picked up this book. You've had enough of 'just getting by', of 'just surviving', and of counting the pennies at the end of each month. Or maybe you've been pretending that everything will turn out okay in the end – the prince will arrive on his charger, you'll receive an unexpected inheritance from someone you never knew, or you'll win the lottery.

Unfortunately, it is your unconscious mind that is running the show, not your conscious mind. It is the part of your brain that manages your breathing, the pumping of your heart and your instinctive reactions to life that is in charge of how much money you have. In order to have more money, you need to influence your unconscious mind. Just *saying* that you want to have more money is not enough. In fact, saying that you want more money only keeps you separated from the money that you want. It keeps you in a position of 'wanting'.

The good news is that the moment you picked up this book, a part of you chose to be wealthy and valued. It's worth taking a second right now to just acknowledge and say 'thank you' to that part because it loves you enough to want the very best for you. (Let's face it, it's about time you started listening to it!) The bad news is that you will have to do something different if you really want to have more money.

> *'Insanity is doing the same thing over and over again and expecting different results.'*
> – **Albert Einstein**

If you have read *How to Become a Money Magnet*, you will understand how a shift in your mindset can transform the world you live in, and the amount of money you are attracting. In fact, since the publication of the book I have been inundated with success stories from readers, and from people I have coached, either individually or on the Money Magnet workshops. It is clear that by shifting your mindset around money, more money can show up easily and often with little or no extra effort!

Maintaining a Money Magnet Mindset

However, I started to notice that, after the initial breakthrough in becoming a Money Magnet, a lot of people then found it hard to actually *maintain* a positive mindset around money. I'd receive calls from people saying things like:

'Marie-Claire, I had an amazing experience after reading your book. I attracted more money effortlessly. I got an unexpected pay rise and I found a new business opportunity! However, since then, things have rather dried up. What can I do to get back on track?'

It seemed that the positive Money Magnet Mindset generated from the book or the workshop wasn't always sustainable. (Interestingly, it did deliver long-term sustainable results for *some* people, and you might have already guessed why this was the case.) I realized that many people were going back to *How to Become a Money Magnet* again and again because every time they read it, there was another breakthrough or realization that helped them to attract more money. However, they were still always coming from a mindset of *fixing* a problem, rather than powerfully *choosing* to be worth more on a daily and long-term basis. I needed to give them a book that showed them how to keep their mindset on track every day – both with their own personal value and with their money.

Let me share a personal example of how important it is to have a *lasting* shift in your mindset whenever you wish to change something in your life. I have always had a somewhat curvaceous figure. Over the years, I have followed a number of diets and various techniques to lose the weight. (Incidentally, did you know that there is a direct link between your weight, your relationships and how much money you have? More on that later!)

Whenever I started a new diet or detox programme, it would be enormously successful. I would easily lose more than 16 kilos (35 pounds) within four weeks. However, the next time I tried that same method I wouldn't lose as much, so I'd switch to an alternative diet. And the first time I tried the alternative diet, I'd lose a lot of weight again, but when I did it a second time it didn't work so well. This kept me in a pattern of always looking for the latest diet to 'fix' my weight problem. (Is any of this sounding familiar to you?)

And the more diets I followed, the more weight I'd put on! It didn't seem fair. I looked at my two sisters – neither of whom had ever been on a diet – and saw they had naturally great figures. I realized I was just exacerbating the problem because I was always coming from the mindset of someone who thinks she has a weight problem to fix!

Do you think you have a money problem? People with money problems tend to look for the next quick 'get rich' solution, swapping one idea for the next and becoming a 'butterfly' – never really settling for one pathway. They also remain focused on fixing the money problem. There are infinite ways to get rich in this world and many more that haven't yet been created – maybe they're waiting for you to discover them?

In fact, there is such an abundance of ideas about the latest way to become a millionaire that you can end up cluttered with information, leaving little space for your own inspiration and value to shine through.

This book gives you the tools to maintain a Money Magnet Mindset for life, and to know that you will always have access to an abundance of resources, including money. It is my intention that this book will also bring you complete peace of mind.

Referring back to the example of dieting, the way to sustain a healthy body is to develop and maintain a healthy mindset around food and your own self-worth – and to practise new habits that will reinforce this new mindset. It will be the decisions you make each mealtime that will make the difference, rather than one big diet that you hope will keep you slim for life. Most importantly, it is about choosing to love yourself every day, just as you are, and then always coming from that point of love for yourself when you are making decisions about food and exercise.

It is exactly the same principle with money. If you want to be financially secure, you'll need to have the mindset of someone who values themself, and who is already financially secure. You'll need to feel good about yourself and your relationship with money. You'll reinforce this healthy mindset through the actions you take each day, which will become good habits. Left alone, your mind will quickly default to its old established patterns, thoughts and beliefs. Take on the recommendations in this book and you will have an effective strategy to keep on track for life.

How to Use This Book

In *How to Become a Money Magnet,* I recommended that you read the entire book and complete 100% of the exercises. Results have shown that those who read the book in this way achieve the most effective and immediate results.

While my first book was focused on you achieving immediate results, this book is designed to give you *lasting results*. If you want to develop a powerful Money Magnet Mindset that will give you long-term results, the best way to use this book is to *read it in the order it's been written, do the prescribed exercises, and adopt the recommended actions!* Once you have read the book in its entirety, I recommend that you then reread the chapters you found the most challenging, and that you then start to incorporate the tools into the discipline of your daily life.

There are three main sections in this book, based on the Money Magnet FAB formula of Focus, Action and Belief. These are the core ingredients in maintaining a Money Magnet Mindset.

FOCUS + ACTION + BELIEF = guaranteed success.

Part 1 is all about **Focus** – if you don't know what you want, or where you're heading, you will become a victim of life's circumstances... and we all know what it feels like to be a victim! Not good!

Part 2 is about **Action**, which I believe is the crucial missing ingredient in many Law of Attraction books. It is when you actually take the action – which often lies outside your comfort zone – that your mindset and personal self-esteem shift and expand and you are consequently able to attract more money.

Part 3 is about **Belief**. To be successful you have to believe in yourself and in what you are doing. This section of the book looks at the ways in which you can maintain that essential self-belief, no matter what happens.

If you want to have more money, you need to manage your mindset around money and your personal value. The really good news is that the Money Magnet Mindset is about so much more than the money. It's about manifesting your dreams. It's about realizing your full worth. It's about becoming a clear channel and sharing your authentic gifts with the world. It's about embracing the real you in all your wonder. You are the miracle. Money is the side effect of you honouring your value and sharing yourself with others.

This book is about you adopting a new way of thinking about yourself, and daily disciplines that reflect your new way of being. We are creatures of habit, though, so it may take some time before you are willing to give up your life and the way you are right now. You have to start from a place of real burning desire to have more money for yourself. Anything less is just wishful thinking. Are you really *committed* to having more money?

> *'How does one become a butterfly?' she asked pensively.*
> *'You must want to fly so much that you give up being a caterpillar.'*

– **Trina Paulus,** *Hope for the Flowers*

Unfortunately, you may also have some unconscious beliefs about money. You may think that the idea of having more money is vulgar, distasteful or greedy. You may have been taught by your parents or your teachers that 'money is the root of all evil', or that 'only the meek and the poor shall enter the kingdom of heaven'.

These unconscious beliefs will get in the way of you being able to express a desire for money – never mind actually attracting more money! In fact, many of the participants on the Money Magnet workshops confess to hiding from their friends the fact that they are even attending one. They admit to feeling embarrassed and ashamed about wanting more money. Can you see how, if *you* felt this way, it might get in the way of you attracting more money?

It is only greedy to want more money if you want it at the expense of someone else. Money is only 'at the root of all evil' if it becomes more important than the person. In other words, it is not money that is to be judged, but the behaviour of the person. Money is a neutral means of exchange. It takes on whatever energy we give it.

So, it might be time for you to embrace and love your money, just as you would want to be embraced and loved yourself. It might be time to love and provide for someone else, just as you would want someone to love and provide for you. It might be time to shout from the rooftops: 'I am a Money Magnet!'

> *'You can have everything in life you want, if you will just help enough other people get what they want.'*
> – **Zig Ziglar**

Once I'd left the corporate world I got interested in what matters most to people. I found that most people want to be loved, and to be happy and fulfilled. I also found that most people need money to pay their bills before they can concentrate on being loved, happy and fulfilled! That was when I created the Money Magnet workshop. It was only when I was looking at ways to reach more people that I went on to write *How to Become a Money Magnet*, and that book is now helping people all over the world.

Money is a measure of your worth in the marketplace. It is what people are prepared to pay you in exchange for what you have to offer. If you want more money it is a symptom that you want to create more value from your life. Acknowledging that you want more, and are prepared to give more, is an important first step in the process of creating a Money Magnet Mindset.

Wake Up to Your Wealth

Most of the people featured in this book reached a point where the voice inside their head was screaming 'Enough! It's time to do something different! I want more money!' This is how it happened to Rachael:

'My wake-up call happened when I was drowning in debt, terribly unhappy – suicidal at times – completely lost and broken. I went to the doctor a complete wreck, which I have never been before. She prescribed antidepressants, and didn't offer counselling or any further help. It was at this point that I lost it. I threw the tablets in the bin after four weeks and said to myself: "There has to be more to life than this! I'm not going to give in to this depression. I will find a healthy alternative for getting well again!"'

Rachael realized in that moment that her true wealth lay within her. She already had all the resources she needed to turn the situation around. All that was missing was the *desire*. Wishing will not bring you more money – it will keep you in a place of hope, despair and quiet resignation. Having a *burning desire* to have more money is the first step to having more money.

> *'Money-consciousness means that the mind has become so thoroughly saturated with the DESIRE for money that one can see oneself already in possession of it.'*
> – **Napoleon Hill**

By the time you finish reading this book, your mind will have all the tools and techniques it needs to embrace more money as your natural birthright. It is then up to you to practise these tools for the rest of your life, so they become habits. Whether you wish to be very rich, or simply to achieve financial freedom (where your income is provided from your assets), it will happen as a result of the small actions you take on a daily basis. These regular actions will train your mind to become one of a Money Magnet!

The real-life stories featured in this book are those of people I have worked with to achieve a Money Magnet Mindset. In some cases I have changed their name, or altered their story slightly to protect their identity, and I'd like to thank each and every one of them for being generous enough to share their experiences with you. I trust that some of the stories will resonate with you, and that you will see you are not alone with the money challenges you currently face. There is always a solution to any problem.

This book is a celebration of what's possible when you believe in yourself and follow your dreams – it is an acknowledgement of your true worth. It's time to relax, read, and open yourself up to your birthright of infinite abundance!

It's time to manifest some more money for yourself! Congratulations on taking the first step!

PART 1

FOCUS

'We have to formulate what we want, be so concentrated on it, so focused on it, and so aware of it, that we lose track of ourselves, we lose track of time, we lose track of our identity.'

– Dr Joseph Dispenza, *The Little Book of Bleeps*

Chapter 1

A World of Infinite Possibilities

'All that we are is the result of what we have thought.'
– Buddha

A basic understanding of quantum physics – and why your thoughts are the key to achieving your desired outcome – is the crucial foundation stone for developing a Money Magnet Mindset. *You* are the creator of your life, as I will explain.

It is human nature to react to life's circumstances and situations. For example, if you went into work tomorrow and found that you were being made redundant, you'd most likely feel upset, and then start to worry about your finances. If you had no savings to fall back on, and no immediate sight of another job, you might even start to panic. You might then become ill. You might start to think that you are not as good as the person who kept their job, or that there's no point in applying for another job if this is what can happen.

You might blame the unbearable manager you had to work for, or the unreasonable number of calls you were expected to make. You might start to think that you didn't want the job anyway! In fact, you're not really sure whether you want a job ever again!

You react to life as if life *happens* to you. You think it isn't down to you that you were made redundant, or that you got behind with your work and didn't bother to put some savings aside. It all just *happened* to you. Life just happens, doesn't it?

The news is full of evidence that there are few jobs available. Everyone is running out of money; the property market is crashing; there is no hope. You might as well give up looking for another job. It all feels so hopeless, and meanwhile, your debt is increasing each day. Who can help you get out of this mess? Who can cheer you up? Where can you find the quickest way to make some money? You need a solution. You are a victim of life's circumstances. Help!

> *'Reasonable men adapt themselves to circumstances, whilst unreasonable men persist in attempting to adapt circumstances to themselves. That is why all progress depends upon the unreasonable man.'*
> – **George Bernard Shaw**

You Are the Creator of Your Life

And then you read a book that explains the Law of Attraction, and how important it is to have positive thoughts. You learn about quantum physics, and about how life only occurs to you as you observe it.

Lynne McTaggart, author of *The Field*, explains that 'in quantum physics... it was discovered, the state of all possibilities of any quantum particle collapsed into a set entity as soon as it was observed or a measurement taken... the consciousness of the observer brought the observed object into being.' This means that the universe as we know it is not a reality of solid objects. Instead, it is in a constant state of flux, and as the observer of your life, it is entirely up to you to choose how it occurs to you. In terms of having more money, this means that on the simplest level you just need to start measuring the money you already have, rather than only seeing what you don't have!

You see what you expect and choose to see, and vice versa. This phenomenon is demonstrated in the 2008 film *Man On Wire*, which tells the true story of tightrope walker Philippe Petit, who performed his daring – and illegal – high-wire routine between the twin towers of New York City's World Trade Center in 1974.

Philippe's feat was an amazing testament to what a human being is capable of, but one of the most remarkable things about it was that none of the pedestrians below could actually see him perform his walk, even though he was doing it right above their heads! Seeing Philippe's friends and family looking up, people stopped in the street and strained to see what they were looking at. It didn't matter how hard they tried to see something, they couldn't physically see Philippe until someone pointed him out to them.

Why was this? Well, it's quite simple: it's impossible for you to see or experience something until you have created it at some level in your mind. If you have no previous experience of something – no idea, concept, or expectation of it – you will be unable to experience a reality in which, say, a tightrope walker crosses a wire between the twin towers in New York.

> ### It doesn't matter how hard you try, you can't see something that you don't expect to see.

Now, if you understand this principle, you can start to see why you will never amass great wealth if, on an unconscious level, you simply don't *see it* as a possibility. For example, you don't see a reality in which you are incredibly wealthy and able to donate freely to worthy causes.

If you've read *How to Become a Money Magnet,* you may have glimpsed a different reality for yourself; I created that within my intention for the book. Now I am handing the instruction manual over to you, so you have the tools and the understanding to constantly keep creating the life you wish for, and the money you desire. If you want to change how your life occurs to you, you need to change how you *think* your life occurs to you. You need to change your thoughts and habits. You need to be clear and focused on what you want, and the life you want will then show up.

Dr Amit Goswami explains this well in *The Little Book of Bleeps*:

> *'It's very easy. Instead of thinking of things as things, you have a habit. We all have a habit of thinking that everything around us is already a thing, existing without my input, without my choice. You have to banish that kind of thinking…*
>
> *'Instead, you really have to recognize that even the material world around us, the chairs, the tables, the room, the carpet,*

the camera included, all of these are nothing but possible movements of consciousness. And I'm choosing moment to moment out of those movements to bring my actual experience into manifestation. This is the only radical thinking that you need to do. But it is so radical. It's so difficult because our tendency is to think that the world is already out there, independent of our experience.

'Quantum Physics has been so clear about it. Heisenberg himself, co-discoverer of Quantum Physics, said atoms are not things. They're only tendencies. So, instead of thinking of things, you have to think of possibilities. There are possibilities of consciousness.'

Be Prepared to See Things Differently

Once upon a time, man believed that the Earth was flat. All the evidence in that reality was that it *was* flat. The more man thought it was flat, the more he saw evidence that it was flat. It appeared to be a fixed reality. Today we know that the Earth is round, but how did the Earth change from being flat to round? Was there a happening in space that expanded the Earth into a round shape? No, we simply changed our minds.

It took one man, the Italian astronomer Galileo Galilei, to be open to a new possibility. Galileo also had the courage to trust what he saw, and to have the passion to promote his fantastic new reality in the face of extreme opposition.

After all, it is *you* who has created your world – just as it is! To change your reality, the first step is to acknowledge your reality and that it is a reality you have created, albeit somewhat unconsciously. Only then can you be open to creating new possibilities, and a new reality.

■ Case Study: Can You Give Up Being Right About Why You Can't Have More Money?

Jane (name changed) called to tell me that she was being forced to do contract work because there are no permanent jobs in HR consultancy in the current market. She was totally convinced of this fact, and her reality meant that in order to work, she had to travel far from home and be in a different geographical location every few months. She was starting to feel unsettled and longed for a permanent job in her home town, ideally with a salary of £50,000.

When I showed Jane how her thoughts were responsible for creating this reality, she became open to creating a reality she desired. Nine weeks after first calling me, Jane attracted what was previously only a dream in her reality: a role in her home town with a salary of exactly £50,000!

When Jane first talked to me, she was adamant that there were no such jobs on the market. Before anything else could be possible, she had to give up being 'right' about her version of the world. If you want more money, and you are convinced that it's impossible for whatever reason, you may have to give up being right about your current reality.

To see your reality from a different perspective, try asking someone else for their opinion and be open to what they say.

You may be so attached to your perceived reality that you need a serious jolt before you wake up to the need for a new one.

This is often what happens when redundancy, divorce or illness occur. These events act as a wake-up call and invite you to question whether this is the life you still choose, or whether you need to start creating a new way of life.

Money Magnet Mindset Tool: Accepting Your Reality

Are you prepared to *accept* the following?

What your reality *is*.

That you may not be right about your reality.

Someone else's perception of your reality.

That there are some areas of your reality you want to change.

That you have the power to create more money, and to make the changes you want.

Open Your Eyes to the Facts

What do I mean when I ask you to 'accept your reality'? Well, I mean that you have to take a good hard look at it and ask yourself:

- What's going on?

- What are the facts?

- What is your current financial situation?

Have you ever watched an overweight woman eating a large portion of greasy chips and wondered why she was doing it? Everyone knows that fatty food makes you fat, and that it's not at all healthy to be overweight. However, the overweight woman isn't looking at the facts that are available to her. She looks in the mirror and convinces herself that she looks okay (if she didn't, she might not even be able to face going out).

To change her reality and become a slim person, she needs, first of all, to accept that she is fat. She needs to get on the scales and measure just how overweight she is. She needs to come face to face with the pain and distress that being fat causes her. When she faces up to what she fears most, the fear will pass and she will finally come to a place of self-acceptance. She will accept herself just as she is. From that point of acceptance she will be open to new possibilities, and able to choose a new reality and a different body shape if she wishes.

Are *you* prepared to really open your eyes to your financial situation and to accept it? By picking up this book, a part of you is ready to confront your money demons once and for all – and to learn how to stay clear of them in the future. Congratulations!

■ Case Study: Facing Up to Your Financial Situation

Felicity (name changed) approached me after I'd given a talk on Money Magnet Mindset to 500 women, asking if she could have a private chat. She was an attractive, elegant, well-dressed lady in her early sixties and my initial impression was that she must be financially successful. If she hadn't explained otherwise, that impression would have remained real for me, and I'm sure that for years, when she looked in the mirror she too saw an attractive, elegant, successful woman, which is why it would have been hard for her to accept her reality.

The truth was that Felicity was in debt to the tune of £250,000. It was a momentous moment for her to face up to this reality, and to choose to share it with someone else. It was the moment she required to open the door to change, and the first essential step on her journey to financial freedom.

Another client, 'Rachel', wrote to me to share her story of facing up to her relationship with money. This is what she said:

'This time last year I was living in London with no job, no money – and I mean no money, it was a choice between feeding myself or paying the rent. I decided to go full-time with my coaching, as I wasn't getting very far with it. I now know why – it was because my relationship with money was negative. I viewed money as the "root of all evil". I had no choice but to claim benefits and I felt ashamed and angry with myself.

'So, I took time out from everything. I did nothing for three months but read, watch movies and meditate. Then I decided to find some work in the corporate world to get more money into my life. I did it to test myself on how I would react to money, and slowly but surely, I began to let go of my old beliefs. I used the methods in How to Become a Money Magnet again and again, and I started to realize that I was going with the flow more and more.

*Don't get me wrong, there are still days when I feel like
I've paused, but the great thing is that I now know what to
do to get unpaused!*

*'I believe in myself more each day. I wouldn't do anything
differently because I wouldn't be who I am today, and the
learning I take from this is to embrace life and money and
not feel guilty. I view money as something to help me, so
why push it away?'*

If you are in debt, it's time to confront your reality and do
something about it. By facing up to the 'monster', things
will become less scary and you will reach the magic moment
of acceptance.

*Accepting that you are totally amazing,
irrespective of the reality you have created
to date, is the key to being able to create the
reality you desire.*

If you have money problems and prefer to ignore your situation
– relying on hope and wishful thinking – nothing will change.
If you spend your time thinking what a terrible person you are
to have got yourself into your financial situation, it will keep
you totally closed to any way of escaping it.

Can you see that for Felicity, trying to think positive thoughts
about money without addressing the reality of her situation
would have been completely ineffective? It was only when she
accepted her situation, without judgement, that she became open
to new possibilities and ways of transforming her circumstances.

Write down your answers to the following questions:

Why are you reading this book?

....

What is your current financial situation?

....

What is not working with your finances?

....

....

Can you accept the facts, without judgement or blame? Can you still choose to love yourself?

....

Once you realize that you can love yourself regardless of your financial situation, you can start to choose a financial reality that you want, rather than the one you thought you deserved!

Money Magnet Mindset Tool: Creating (Or Not) Creating More Money, Part 1

List all the reasons why you think you can't have more money right now.
(For example: 'The economy is in such a bad state', or 'Salary levels are too low', or 'I don't have the right qualifications.' And don't pretend you don't have any reasons!)

....

....

....

....

....

....

You *must* complete this before moving on to Part 2 of the exercise.

Money Magnet Mindset Tool: Creating (Or Not) Creating More Money, Part 2

Now answer these two questions:

Can you give up being 'right' about why you can't have more money?

....

....

Can you see why you may have chosen, albeit unconsciously, not to have more money?

....

....

The answers may not come easily at this point, but keep returning to this tool until you start to get some clarity. As you read on, and learn how other people have also limited the amount of money they have, you will find it easier to answer them.

You must respond to question one before you can really answer the second question. Keep coming back until you can give up being right about why you don't have more money.

Can You Give Up Being 'Right' About Why You Can't Earn More Money?

Let's look at some possible responses to this question. You might say that there's a fixed salary for your job, or that you can't do anything else, or that no one is getting a pay rise and it's not a good climate to be making money. Can you see that, whatever reasons you come up with, they may not be true or valid? After all, history shows us there are more millionaires created during financial depressions than during boom times, and there are plenty of people making money right now.

If you are looking for bad news, and reasons why you can't have more money, you will find them.

Being 'right' will keep you in a prison that you yourself have created. If Galileo had believed he was right about the Earth being flat, he would never have been open to the new possibility of it being round. If you are 'right' about how dreadful your situation is, you will stay closed to any possibility of turning it around.

■ Case Study: Expand Your Earning Possibilities

Rishpal worked as a personal fitness trainer. In her world, fitness trainers only earned a certain amount of money, and their earnings were limited by the hours they worked. She could have remained convinced that there was no way she could earn more money as a personal trainer, but then she would never have been open to a new way of doing things.

Instead, Rishpal opened herself to the possibility of earning much more money in personal fitness training than her hours would physically allow. At first, she hadn't a clue how this might happen, but then she had the idea of creating a company to train people to become personal trainers. Now, with FitAchieveTrain, there is no limit to the amount of money she can earn in the field of personal training, and she is helping many more people to achieve their dreams than when she was working on a one-to-one basis.

When people attend the one-day Money Magnet workshop, they see a new possibility for themselves. Almost immediately, they start to attract more money. It is part of the new reality they get to see for themselves on the day. And it's not just real for *them,* either – other people on the course witness that they have become Money Magnets. It is their new identity and it occurs as reality. After the workshop though, something goes wrong in their lives – maybe a deal doesn't work out, or they receive an unexpected bill – and they forget that they are the creator of their lives. They relapse into the role of victim.

That's why it's important you have the tools to maintain the Money Magnet Mindset on a daily basis.

Can You See Why You May Have Chosen, Albeit Unconsciously, Not to Have More Money?

Question two asks why you might have created such a reality for yourself. Why would you choose to have a certain level of money, or even no money, coming in? The key is to look at how you benefit, on an unconscious level, from not having much money.

When I first started in sales, I couldn't sell a thing! That was my reality. Inside I knew that I was meant to be in sales, but no matter how hard I tried, I was the worst salesperson in the company! It's a terrible feeling to be in sales and to find yourself on the bottom rung of the sales performance table. If you've started your own company and are facing the prospect of selling for the first time, you may have a similar sense of trepidation!

Imagine the scene. Every Monday morning, 60 salespeople, most of them men, would gather in the southern offices of a large US corporation to announce what they had sold the previous week, and what they promised to sell the following week.

The first week I proudly announced that I would make one sale. But when the Monday arrived, I had to announce a big fat zero, with a firm promise that I would make one sale the following week. The third Monday arrived and I had to announce another big fat zero, with another promise of a sale the following week. My voice was beginning to waver a little by then. By the twelfth week, I just wanted the ground to swallow me up rather than face 59 salespeople with the shame and embarrassment of yet another zero! I felt a complete failure and I couldn't see any possible way of turning the situation around.

I was so determined to be successful. I'd joined the best company in the business for sales training; I had the best team to support me; I had approached all the top salespeople and asked them how they'd done it. I'd read all the books and listened to the Zig Ziglar tapes. I was working all the hours I could, determined to show that I really was doing my best, and yet all I had to show for my efforts, and the long hours invested, was still a big fat zero!

> *Remember, it doesn't matter how hard you work, if some part of you is resisting success, you need to recognize it, accept it, and then let it go so you can have more money.*

Have you ever found yourself working all the hours you can, and yet still only ever achieving a minimum level of income and never experiencing a breakthrough in your performance and results? It can be exhausting; I was exhausted! Then I finally reached the point where enough was enough! I'd come face to face with the reality of my situation and I didn't like it one bit!

How I Accepted My Reality

I asked myself the two questions in the Money Magnet Mindset Tool above, and this was my response:

I thought I couldn't sell because I lacked confidence and was no good at it, and because I hadn't actually achieved any sales. When I gave up being 'right' about that, I realized it wasn't necessarily true. As soon as I gave up my version of reality, I began to see evidence of why I could be good at it – excellent training, great team support, limitless training resources, etc. I also reckoned I wouldn't have been employed if the company didn't believe in me. I looked back at other times when I'd been a salesperson and had been really good at selling.

So why would I have created a reality in which I was failing as a salesperson? There had to be a benefit if my unconscious mind was protecting me from being good at sales. This was when I remembered an early job I'd had as a Saturday sales assistant for a menswear retail chain.

Every Saturday morning, before the shop doors were opened, the manager would take us all over to a particular model of suit (it was a different one each Saturday). He would then tell us that if we sold any units of that particular suit, we would receive a huge bonus, equivalent to almost twice our whole day's pay! Imagine the scene. Man comes into the shop to buy a suit... which one am I going to recommend he tries on? Man tries on two different suits. Which one will I tell him he looks best in? Absolutely – the one that pays me the bonus! Now, I'd like to think that I never sent a customer out of the shop with a suit that looked terrible on him, but even so, my primary motivation had been to earn the bonus.

Years later, I am trying to be really good at sales when I realize I've picked up an unconscious belief about salespeople – and it's not a good one! Clearly, I thought, to be a good salesperson, you have to be devious, manipulative and prepared to lie.

Can you see how my unconscious mind was working especially hard to protect me from becoming such a nasty person? It didn't matter how hard I worked, or what expert advice I received, I was committed to making sure I never succeeded in sales!!

This belief that salespeople are essentially nasty liars nestled in my unconscious mind for years, and it was only when I objectively questioned my lack of success at sales, and why this could be, that I became aware of it. I could see I had 'created' myself as unsuccessful at sales in order to be a nice, honest person.

By having zero sales and zero commission, I was 'proving' to myself that I was a good and honest person. How many people do you know who value being a good, spiritual human being over and above being financially successful? They don't realize that they can be a good, spiritual person *and* be financially successful! In fact, the more you serve others, the more successful you become.

My unconscious mind, with the information it had, was doing its best to protect me from becoming a devious, manipulative liar, and it was doing a great job! It was keeping me safe by hiding all the evidence that would label me a salesperson. And the side effect was no sales, no commission and no money!

Now, in order to free myself from this limiting belief, all I had to do was shine a spotlight on it, understand where it came from – my first sales experience at 17 – and realize that the belief was not necessarily true. I could now look for evidence of good salespeople who were making a real difference in the world with their offerings. Typical examples would be British entrepreneurs Sir Richard Branson and Sir Alan Sugar. In collecting new, positive beliefs about salespeople, I was able to create a new reality in which being a salesperson was a fantastic thing!

All beliefs are, at some level, made up. So if I could make up a limiting belief about salespeople, I could also make up an empowering one. If I could create a reality in which I was not successful, I could also create one in which I was successful.

So I chose to believe that I was good at sales, and in no time at all my results started to take off. I got promoted, and within a few years I was delivering £1million sales revenue each month.

> *If all beliefs are made up, it makes sense to make up ones that will empower you!*

Money Magnet Mindset Tool: Clearing Your Limiting Beliefs

Now it's your turn to see how you may be holding yourself back from financial success. Take these five steps to clear your unconscious blocks around having more money.

Step 1: Ask yourself how you could possibly be benefiting from the experience of having less money.
(For example: 'I don't have to work so hard and I have more time to devote to a loving relationship.')

Step 2: Look for when you first had a similar experience, and what you made it mean.
(For example: 'When I worked really hard in a previous job, I earned lots of money but I didn't have time for a relationship and my health suffered. So I thought that to have lots of money, I had to work hard and then suffer.')

Step 3: Recognize that any belief is just made up, and therefore not true.
(For example: 'It's not true that you have to work hard and suffer to earn money.')

Step 4: Create a new, more empowering belief that supports you.
(For example: 'I can believe that it's possible to earn more money easily and effortlessly and still have plenty of time to spend with my loved ones.')

Step 5: Collect evidence to support that new belief.
(For example, 'Property investors, internet marketers and network marketers are examples of people who create an income that is disproportionate to the hours they work.)

Unconscious limiting beliefs get in the way of you creating the life and the money you want for yourself. You can't attract more money if you have an underlying belief that you *shouldn't* have any more money, for whatever 'valid' reason. It can be difficult to uncover your own unconscious beliefs, due to the fact that you are unconscious of them! So don't worry if, after using the steps above, you haven't yet uncovered your own limiting beliefs around money. Chapter 2 takes this further and, prompted by a few more stories, I'm sure you will uncover your unconscious blocks around money.

I recommend, however, that you return to this chapter, and the five steps above, whenever you are feeling blocked around money. There can be many layers to your belief system, and it is only when you clear the ones that don't serve you that you can create a new possibility in your world.

How about creating the possibility of money flowing easily and effortlessly into your bank accounts when you do what you love to do best?

MONEY MAGNET MINDSET HABITS: START A DAILY 'CREATE MY LIFE' JOURNAL

- Each morning, write down what you plan should happen that day. Look at specific outcomes – for example, one visit to the gym, one phone call to mother, two new clients, £10,000 sales revenue. If you want to talk to a particular person, write down their name. We're not looking for long lists: just jot down the key essentials that you intend should happen for the day to count as a great one in your life… and then take a moment to SMILE as you consider the great day ahead of you!

- At the end of the day, review your notes and congratulate yourself on your creation. Observe any particular successes, and acknowledge how you created them.

- If something didn't go according to plan during the day, take time to ask yourself how you could have been responsible for it. Were you 100% committed to the specified outcome? At first this might feel strange, but with practice you'll start to realize that you really can have the life and the money of your dreams if you accept your role as the creator of your reality.

Keep challenging your limiting beliefs around money:

- Write down and challenge any limiting beliefs that you hold about money.

- Physically cross out the limiting beliefs, or burn the piece of paper.

- Write down your new empowering beliefs about money.

- Start looking for evidence to support your new empowering beliefs.

Chapter 2

Clear Your Mind

'It's not the daily increase but daily decrease.
Hack away at the unessential.'
– Bruce Lee

So, the good news is that you are the creator of your life and the amount of money in it. Your thoughts create your reality. If you believe that you will never have enough money, you will never have enough money, no matter how many times you say otherwise. But if you genuinely believe that you will always succeed, irrespective of the external evidence, then you will.

When American business magnate Donald Trump was $900million in personal debt, I'll bet he didn't succumb to the 'poor me' syndrome. In his mind he was still worth so much more, and with that type of mindset, and his formidable deal-making skills, he was able to turn things around... and not for the first time either!

So, how do you maintain a healthy Money Magnet Mindset through the bad times as well as the good? Well, there are two answers to that question:

1.   The positive Money Magnet Mindset must be programmed into you from an early age, and reinforced through your subsequent actions.

2.   You learn how to clear your mind of limiting beliefs and train it to stay focused on what you want, and not what you *don't* want.

Donald Trump had a privileged upbringing and that may account, to some extent, for his Money Magnet Mindset. This early belief was then reinforced by his actions, and the amazingly successful deals he achieved. The beliefs in *your* unconscious mind were formed as a result of where you were born, your parents' beliefs about money, your teachers' beliefs about you, and the many experiences in your life to date and what you made them mean. British entrepreneur Sir Alan Sugar didn't have a privileged upbringing, but there are lots of examples of people who, like him, have felt driven to become rich in order to escape the type of life they experienced growing up.

It is this programming of your beliefs about money, often from an early age, that will set the level of money you allow yourself, irrespective of how hard you work. No matter how much you earn, spend, and save, you will always end up with roughly the same amount of money. The only way to change this is to change the programming in your mind. And in my experience, there are lots of beliefs that you may wish to transform. Clearing out old limiting beliefs, and building new empowering ones, is an ongoing commitment if you want to become rich and stay rich.

What is Your Current Level of Money Magnetism?

So, how can you gauge your current level of Money Magnetism? That's easy: look in your bank account! You may consciously want to have more money in your bank account, but it is your unconscious thoughts and beliefs that dictate how much is actually in there at the end of each month. Your unconscious mind is the part that is managing the money in your life, and no doubt keeping you safe from having too much of it!

> *This is the Money Mindset problem: if your thoughts about money are unconscious, you are not conscious of them. If you are not conscious of them, you cannot change them. If you cannot change them, you are destined to remain at more or less the same income level all your life.*

If you are programmed to believe that all wealthy people are arrogant and selfish, your unconscious mind will make sure that you never become wealthy because it wants to keep you safe. It doesn't matter that your conscious mind wants nothing more than to be a millionaire, it is your unconscious mind that's in charge.

> *You need to become conscious of the unconscious limiting beliefs you hold about money, so you can then change these beliefs.*

The best way that I've found to awaken people to the beliefs they are holding in their unconscious is to tell them real-life stories of other people's unconscious limiting beliefs. My intention is that they will recognize a belief as one of their own if the story resonates with them, or, in just hearing the story of another, they may have an insight for themselves.

It is the unconscious mind that we address in the Money Magnet workshops, so allow me to share with you a few stories from them. When reading the rest of this chapter, please stay alert to any limiting beliefs you uncover for yourself which you didn't realize you had. It's a good idea to have a pen and a journal or notebook to hand to record any thoughts that come up for you.

Limiting Belief: 'If You Don't Have any Money, You Can Protect Yourself from the Pain of Losing it'

Caren came along to a Money Magnet workshop just to keep her friend company. She was in her fifties, happily married, and her children had recently left home for university. Caren had no real income of her own and to fill the time now available to her, and to connect with other women in a similar position, she and a friend had created a website for women gardeners. The website had no membership subscriptions, or any other obvious ways to attract money. Caren said that, in an ideal world, she would love to start earning her own money again, independent of her husband, but she couldn't really see how that would be possible.

During the workshop, Caren was taken back in her mind to a time when she was six years old and she was woken in the middle of the night by her parents. Told to grab her favourite toy, she was then bundled into the car and the family drove away under the cover of night. She never saw that home again. It was a six-year-old's experience of her father going bankrupt. Now much older and married, she also remembered when her husband had gone bankrupt with his business. In that moment, she remembered all the feelings of shame and embarrassment associated with this experience.

It became immediately clear to Caren why she had no income of her own. Her unconscious mind had taken the two most traumatic experiences of her life and concluded that they were both to do with money. Her mind had then created a 'story' of its own, the conclusion of which was that having money was 'dangerous'. The unconscious message was this: once you have money, the next thing will be to experience feelings of deep loss and pain.

On some level, Caren's mind did everything to avoid having money, as it knew from past experience that the next thing that happens is that you lose it, and then experience huge trauma. By the end of the workshop, Caren felt emotionally exhausted, but she looked as though she had lost ten years or more in age just by releasing a story that she'd been holding on to for years.

Money Magnet Miracle

Within one week of the Money Magnet workshop, *without her doing anything different*, Caren's business had attracted a major UK-wide advertiser willing to pay her a substantial sum of money to feature on her website. Caren had become a Money Magnet! She went from strength to strength financially. The next time I saw her, I didn't recognize her as the anxious, timid lady from the workshop. In her place was a confident, stunning businesswoman who was clearly now very successful and making a difference to others with her offering.

If you have had any experience of bankruptcy or financial hardship within your family, take a look at how this may have impacted your relationship with money. It is enough to recognize this possible limiting belief, because once it is recognized by your conscious mind, it can no longer run your life from an unconscious level. You will have the power to choose things differently, and to become a master of your thoughts and beliefs.

What you focus on expands. Caren chose to focus on 'money', rather than 'no money', and the more she focused on money, the more money she attracted!

Money Magnet Mindset Tool: Exploring Your Parents' Relationship with Money

Describe the relationship your parents had with money. For example, were they savers or spenders? Was there always plenty of money, or never quite enough? Did you learn good money habits at a young age, like saving? Did you rebel against your parents' teachings once you left home?

Limiting Belief: 'Wealth Corrupts a Person's True Nature'

Some people say they want more money, but if it involves giving up a well-entrenched belief, it's incredible how much resistance can come up.

Alison came to a Money Magnet workshop with a friend. She was in her early thirties and in the previous year had left work to start her own business. The business was doing well, which was no doubt down to Alison's hard work and tireless networking. The problem was that she just couldn't seem to get beyond a certain income level.

On the workshop Alison unwittingly uncovered her resistance to wealth when she uttered the words: 'The last person I'd want to be like is my sister!' This was said with such strong emotion that I decided to explore the story. Alison couldn't bear her sister, Claire. The problems had started when Claire married a wealthy man. Alison's perception was that Claire, now with money, had transformed into an ugly-minded person and she couldn't bear to be in her company, let alone be like her!

It was clear to everyone in the room that Alison had an unconscious belief that having more money would mean she'd transform, like her sister, into a not very nice person. It didn't matter how hard she worked, she would never become a wealthy, successful businessperson with a belief like that running the show! My recommendation was that Alison make peace with her sister.

Unfortunately, Alison resisted doing this. Remember, we all like to be right about our beliefs, and she didn't want to give up believing that her sister was a bad person who had been corrupted by wealth. Instead, she simply decided to work even harder on her business, clocking up 20-hour days and applying every marketing tactic she could think of. Six months later she called me in tears. She'd missed a mortgage payment. That was the final straw and her moment of 'enough is enough!' It felt bad enough to make her willing to address the one thing that would make a difference – her relationship with her sister.

Money Magnet Miracle

At the *exact moment* Alison made peace with her sister, monies were transferred from a customer's account into her business bank account – these were invoices that had remained unpaid for months. The timing of the transfers was nothing short of miraculous. In embracing the love she had for her sister, Alison was able to create a new, empowering belief that wealthy people are loved for who they are, irrespective of what is in their bank account. She has since received an offer from someone wanting to buy her company!

Money Magnet Mindset Tool: Identifying Your Attitude to Wealthy People

Think of three wealthy people and then complete the following table.

Name of Wealthy Person	Your Thoughts About this Person

When describing the person, did you mention their money?

What do you think of them as a human being?

What are your first thoughts when you hear about someone becoming wealthy overnight?

Would you want to be like them in any way?

Limiting Belief: 'Never Trust a Salesperson'

In the last chapter, I described how I formed a limiting belief about salespeople. Until I identified this belief, I just couldn't achieve any sales.

Can you see that if you want to have more money, but for some reason you don't like the idea of selling or being a salesperson, this is likely to block your chances of success? If you are listening to the little voice that is telling you that 'you'll never be any good at sales', or that you'd rather be 'broke' for a month than ever be described as a 'salesperson', this next exercise is especially for you!

Money Magnet Mindset Tool: Learning to Love Salespeople

Describe your experience of salespeople.
(For example: 'They make me feel pressured.')

....

....

What do you think about salespeople?
(For example: 'They are pushy and selfish.')

....

....

What would be the worst thing about someone describing *you* as a salesperson?
(For example: 'You are greedy.')

....

....

Now think of the last time you were delighted to buy something from a salesperson (for example, a car or a holiday). What was it about the salesperson that made the experience so pleasurable?
(For example: 'They got me excited!')

....

....

If I knew of a one-day workshop that could guarantee an increase in your earnings, you'd want to know more about it, right? You'd want to know how to get on it, how much it costs, where it's being held, who else will be attending, and so on. However, can you see that if I kept quiet about the workshop for fear you might think I'm 'selling' it to you, you would be deprived of a golden opportunity to increase the amount of money in your life?

Salespeople offer you opportunities. Without salespeople you would stay doing what you've always done. Salespeople have the courage and generosity to share new opportunities with you – whether they are opportunities to look good in the latest car or to invest in yourself and your life with the latest workshop or coaching programme. It is up to you to choose what's right for you. Learn to love salespeople. They can bring colour to your life, and good salespeople are passionate leaders who inspire others. They are fun people to be around.

What is your new, empowering belief about selling/salespeople?

....

....

Limiting Belief: 'I Can't be Trusted with Money'

Can you remember your very first experience of money? How old were you?

I was about seven and my first experience was stealing coins from my parents' cash box at home. I was really good at it! I took as much as I could each time, but never so much that anyone would notice. Nobody ever did notice – it was another 40 years before I finally confessed to my mother!

The problem was that, although no one knew about me stealing the money, on some level I now had a belief that I couldn't be trusted with money. The impact this had on my relationship with myself, and my relationship with money, was significant.

One of my first sales jobs was as a Saturday sales assistant in a trendy women's clothing retailer. I was paid £6 for a day's work, and I would spend the whole time working out which item of clothing I was going to spend my £6 on! As soon as I had the money in my hand, I'd spent it – before I'd even left the store!

Years later, the same pattern continued, but the sums were larger! I might be paid £10,000 for one month's work, and then I would find an original painting to buy for £8,000. My salary increased to a six-figure sum and I went out and bought myself a brand new apartment! As long as I had the unconscious belief that 'I couldn't be trusted with money', I was getting rid of the money as fast as I could!

You can imagine the consequences: I had no savings! My one saving grace was that some of the money was spent on property. It also meant I was valuing everyone else over and above myself. My self-worth was impacted by this story about myself, and as a result, I was giving my money to everyone but myself!

Money Magnet Mindset Tool: Exploring Your First Experience of Money

Describe your first experience of money.

....

What did you make it mean about you and money?

....

....

How did it affect the way you are now with money?

....

....

Can you change your mind right now about this belief?

....

If, in reading my story, you've remembered something similar in your own life, that's good. Usually, at least half the room at a Money Magnet workshop admit to having stolen money when they were a child.

Part of being a child is to test the boundaries. Yes, you may have stolen money as a child and yes, at that point in time you could not be trusted with money. However, unless you have evidence that you are still stealing money, it is time to let go of this out-of-date belief that is not serving you.

It is time to look at ways that you *can* be trusted with your money. For example, do you always look for the best deals when travelling? Do you check your bill in a restaurant? Do you put money aside each month for your savings? This book will introduce you to many more ways that you can start to create a more loving and trusting relationship with money. It is time to create a new empowering belief about how much you now trust yourself with money, and to reinforce it with some new money habits.

Limiting Belief: 'I Don't Want to Do What My Parents Tell Me to Do'

Many of your unconscious beliefs were installed at a young age, and the child lives on in your mind until you decide to let them go and grow up. Look to see where the child's viewpoint is still having an impact on your life, and resolve now to let it go. You are an adult and you can choose only the beliefs that empower you.

For example, my parents always had enough money for the important things in life – like my school education, my first ever skiing holiday with the school at 18, and the gorgeous house we lived in. But the general feeling was that money wasn't plentiful. It was tightly managed and my parents were very careful with their money. As soon as I left home, one of the ways I asserted my new-found freedom was to spend money frivolously. I could now do what I wanted, and spending money was one of the easiest ways to express my freedom from parental influence. And of course I had the belief that the important things would always be taken care of!

When I realized that my spending habits were rooted in a rebellion against my parents, I knew it was about time I grew up and took responsibility for my own life! The best way I knew to acknowledge my parents, and to be able to care for them in their old age, was to follow the good money habits they had taught me and my siblings.

Limiting Belief: 'It's Love or Money – There's Not Enough Time for Both!'

My father lost his job when I was 12. I still remember coming back from school to find him at home, and knowing instinctively that something was very wrong. Is it really a coincidence, I wonder, that his daughters became entrepreneurs, forsaking the 'unreliable' world of regular paid employment?

My parents already had one business of their own, a caravan site behind our house, and so my father decided to set up a wine shipping business. My memories of growing up from then on were of living with my parents' business, and my parents working all hours in it. It seemed to me that they were always in the office and had no time to be with us. I made that mean that earning money was more important than being with people you love.

Years later, I find myself running my own business and complaining that I don't have any time to spend with my loved ones! It's not true! I can choose to work when I wish. I've simply created an unconscious belief from my earlier experience that when you work for yourself, you have to work all the hours you can just to earn enough money to survive! There's no time left in the day for anything or anyone else.

The truth is, of course, that my father did very well in his business, and he was always at hand, working from home. His business provided us with all we needed growing up, as well as a secure financial future for him and my mother. He chose to spend time on the business as a way of expressing his love for us, and out of a burning desire to provide for his family. I now see that my business is an expression of my love, and I choose to spend lots of time doing what I love.

Limiting Belief: 'I Have to Work Hard to Earn Money'

This is a very common belief. On some level it's good: the harder you work, the more money you'll earn. However, there is a limit to how many hours you can work in a day, and it doesn't sound much like a fun way to live your life! If you think you *have* to work hard to earn money, it might put you off wanting more money on an unconscious level. You want the money but you'll shy away from the work that you imagine must be involved in making £1million. If you think that you *have* to work hard to earn your money, what will you do when the work becomes easy?

When I was a sales director, I put the hours in to create a well-trained and motivated salesforce. The problem was, having put the work in at the start, there was little left for me to do other than report the results and oversee the team. I got bored. I was being paid a good salary and I was delivering the results, but I was no longer having to work hard to earn the money.

When you have a belief that you have to work hard to earn money, sooner or later you can't sustain earning a lot of money without having to do much work. I started to feel like a fraud. It was no surprise, looking back, that I chose to walk from a job that paid me handsomely and gave me a luxurious lifestyle. I walked because I was no longer working hard, and so, on an unconscious level, I couldn't accept my salary.

Contrast this with my current lifestyle, where I earn money easily doing what I love most and making a real difference to people through my coaching and workshops. I have learnt to work SMART, where sending one simple email can generate lots of income and still leave me with time to spend with my loved ones.

A more empowering belief would be to recognize that money is an exchange of value, and the more value you give, the more you will receive.

Money Magnet Mindset Tool: Exploring Your Relationship with Money

Tick the statements that resonate most with you:

'Money is dirty.'

'Money is the root of all evil.'

'I can't be trusted with money.'

'I'm hopeless with money.'

'I have to work hard to earn money.'

'I don't want to be rich, I just want enough to get by.'

'When you get money, the odds are that you'll lose it.'

'Money is all about power.'

'It's rude to talk about money.'

Other (please specify) ....

....

....

Limiting Belief: 'Money is Dirty and it's Rude to Talk about Money'

British people are probably more comfortable talking about sex than money! One of the biggest breakthroughs people get on the Money Magnet workshops is being able to talk openly about money.

Money taps into the secret of your values. There is no hiding from how much you value yourself when the bank statements are on the table.

Your parents may have told you that it's impolite to talk about how much you earn. Companies often forbid their employees from exchanging salary details, and this creates feelings of distrust and suspicion among the staff. It also encourages the feeling that money, and any mention of money, is a bad thing. Every person is worthy as a human being, so we ask ourselves: 'How can we judge somebody, or even ourselves, for having more or less money than someone else?'

Money Magnet Mindset Tool: Talking About Money

Look at the following scenarios and ask yourself how comfortable you are in them. Give yourself marks out of ten for each of them:

Asking your boss for a pay rise. ..... /10

Asking a friend for a loan. ..... /10

Charging someone for your time. ..... /10

Increasing your prices. ..... /10

Lending money to a friend. ..... /10

Borrowing money from your parents. ..... /10

Discussing your will with your family. ..... /10

Planning investments with your partner. ..... /10

Giving someone a tip for good service.	..... /10
Not giving them a tip for poor service!	..... /10
Telling someone that you won't be buying an item because the price is too high.	..... /10
Asking for a discount.	..... /10
Negotiating payment terms.	..... /10

How did you do? Can you see that if you are uncomfortable even *talking* about money, you may have problems *attracting* more of it? The person who is happy enough to talk money will be the one who gets the pay rise or the best deal.

If you want to find people who are comfortable talking about money, go into a room full of wealthy businesspeople, property investors or millionaires. They can talk about money easily and comfortably. They understand that it is simply a vehicle – a currency that represents an exchange of value. They understand that the person with the most money is usually the one who has found the best way to serve the most people. There is no other hidden meaning; they have nothing to hide. They are comfortable with their true worth – even proud of it.

> *Your wealth reflects the size of your contribution to society, and how much society values that contribution.*

Limiting Belief: 'Women Earn Less than Men'

There is plenty of evidence to support the belief that women earn less than men. However, there are also plenty of examples in which a woman's pay outstrips a man's. Your version of reality depends on what you are focused on.

I'm often asked by journalists to comment on the difference in pay scales that still exists between the sexes. *'Why is it that women are still paid less than men?'* is the most common question. Others include: *'Don't you think that the government should do more to bring it into balance?'* and *'Shouldn't employers be forced to give women equal pay?'* and, the worst one of all: *'Aren't men at fault for accepting more money than women?'*

Consider the following scenario. A pay freeze is announced in your company. It is to last for a whole year and no one can expect to receive a pay rise during that time. How would you react? Would you sigh and accept that you are stuck on the same money for at least another year? Or would you immediately start to look for another job? Or would you stride into your boss's office and confidently deliver a proposal as to why you should be considered as an exception to the rule?

For many women, the idea of the 'stay-at-home, obedient women' is still part of their consciousness. For others, the child who learnt at a young age to obey the parent is still in their psyche. So, in this situation, there will be a somewhat resigned acceptance of their fate, stemming from a respect for authority, a willingness to serve others, or a fear of standing out from the crowd.

Now, just imagine that you *knew* you deserved a pay rise. You knew that you had delivered so much value and commitment that it would be only natural for you to receive more money, irrespective of company policy. Would you be comfortable asking for it? Yes, of course you would. As a boss in a company,

I can share that we take note of the people who ask for a pay rise. If there is a limited pot of money, and work levels are roughly equal, we will award the money to those who have made a point of asking for it, whether that is right or wrong. Most human beings will take the easiest option.

In one of my first jobs as a salesperson, I thought that all you had to do was keep your head down and work hard and you would be rewarded with a pay rise. Wrong! You have to *ask* for what you want! And if you're not comfortable talking about money, or your personal worth, you're never going to be the one who gets a pay rise – unless you just get lucky. That's what you call being a victim of life's circumstances.

Let's be clear: you are not a victim. You have the power to choose the life you want. You have the power to attract the income you desire. The first steps are to look at the value you offer, to make friends with money, and to start talking about it!

Money Magnet Mindset Tool: The 'Mirror' Pitch

Think of a conversation you could have about money (asking for a pay rise, or charging someone for your services, for example). Then set aside some time to do this exercise:

Step 1: Find yourself a mirror and practise asking the person in the mirror for the money that you want.

Step 2: Keep practising until the person in the mirror says 'yes'. Then go and have the conversation in real life.

Bonus exercise: multiply the amount you ask for by ten, and then do the exercise again. Then ask for double your original amount in reality.

Limiting Belief: 'I'm Not Good Enough'

This is the limiting belief that comes up the most on the Money Magnet workshops. In fact, it comes up so often that if I had to choose one belief that applies to everyone, at some level, this would be it. Does it apply to you? Are you ready to let go of it now?

Some people use the feeling that they are 'not good enough' to drive them forward and to earn lots of money. But as a strategy, this is flawed. At what level of money do you become 'good enough'? The belief that you are never good enough stays, irrespective of income, and in many cases it will be the underlying cause of a future loss of money.

My mother was *not* happy when I picked all the bluebells in our garden – every single one of them! I was seven years old and I understood in that moment that I was a bad and naughty girl who was being punished by being sent to her room. I was 'not good enough', and I was devastated! The emotional feeling I experienced lodged itself into my unconscious mind.

I am now way past 40 and I can see that this particular incident was just that – an incident in time. I was always 'good enough'. Any meaning I attached to this one isolated incident was made up by a seven-year-old child. It has absolutely no validity in how I view myself today. Any story that you have about yourself, and why you're not good enough, has no validity either. It's not true – it's a story you made up about yourself. Do you really want your life to be governed by a story that you made up as a child? I thought not. It's even a bit ridiculous, isn't it?

You were born good enough. You were born as the most precious commodity in the world. There is only one of you, and you are the best 'you' that you can be.

Not being good enough is all about 'me'. When you stop looking at your belly button and look up to see who you can help, you will forget that you're 'not good enough' and you will become more than good enough for yourself and others. When you accept another person's acknowledgement of the good that you provide for them, you will then accept that you are 'good enough' in your own eyes.

Money Magnet Mindset Tool: Changing Your Personal Story

Who told you that you weren't good enough? How old were you?

....

Is the reason why you were 'not good enough' then really valid today?

....

Who decides if you are 'good enough'?

....

What would you do if you knew that you were 'good enough'?

....

Limiting Belief: 'Nobody in Our Family Ever Makes it'

Tania raised her hand at a talk I was giving in which I was inviting people to share the limiting beliefs that were holding them back from being successful in life. Tania's story was that her dad had tried to be a success in business. He had tried several times to make it, and each time he had failed. Then he died, leaving his family in debt. Tania's belief was that if her father hadn't made a success in business, then how could *she* ever be successful?

Sounds plausible? Actually, to me it sounded more like an excuse, but to be fair to Tania, she had only just recognized this belief at a conscious level. Until then, the belief had been 'running the show' in her unconscious. Now, normally it is enough for you to recognize your limiting belief for you to then choose a more powerful belief. But Tania was struggling to give this one up, and I suspected that she was still angry about her father's failure. She hadn't forgiven him.

There are plenty of reasons to cling onto your limiting beliefs. They can be the best justification for not taking action, and for not having the courage to follow your dreams. Tania was convinced that she was right.

By now you will be starting to recognize *your* biggest limiting belief to having more money. It might be any one of those mentioned above, a variation of one of them, or a completely different one, uncovered in the stories of others. By all means indulge yourself in your belief for a while longer, but when you are ready, I suggest that you reframe it into a more positive belief.

Addressing Tania, and her belief that her father was a failed businessman, I invited her to look at her father from a different perspective. The majority of people work in a 9-5 job for most of their lives. There is nothing wrong with this, of course, and it is what most of us have been educated to do. I pointed out to Tania that it takes real courage for someone to go against the norm and to dare to follow their dreams. Most successful entrepreneurs fail numerous times, and often quite spectacularly, before they succeed. Instead of seeing her father as a failure, I encouraged Tania to look at him as a hero who dared to believe in himself when others didn't.

Tania's shoulders relaxed and there were tears in her eyes as she released all the anger and frustration she had invested in this belief. She seemed to lose ten years in age as she let go of the tension. Others in the room had similar reactions as they related to what they were hanging onto, and freed themselves from the imagined hurt and frustration within them.

Money Magnet Mindset Tool: Reframing Your Limiting Belief

Write down your most powerful belief about why you don't have more money.
(For example: 'My parents were poor.')

....

....

....

How could this become an empowering belief that will help you earn more money?

(For example: 'A high percentage of successful entrepreneurs come from impoverished families.')

....

....

Note: If you are struggling with this exercise, ask a friend or a coach to help you.

Madeleine was at the same conference as Tania, and she was quick to put her hand up. Actually, to be precise, Madeleine was in a wheelchair and it was her assistant who beckoned me to come to Madeleine. Her really strong belief was that she had to die in order to make money! For me, this was a new variation on the more common belief that 'money only comes to me when my loved ones die'.

See if you can reframe Madeleine's limiting belief before I tell you what I came up with:

....

I suggested to Madeleine that she focus on the type of legacy she would like to leave when she died. After all, we are all going to die one day, and if you have a belief that you'll receive money after your death, why not make good provision for what you leave behind? Of course, you could also reframe Madeleine's belief by looking at death as change, and then looking to see what major change was needed for her to make money. There is no right or wrong way to reframe a belief, as long as the new belief is an empowering one.

MONEY MAGNET HABITS: TRANSFORM YOUR BELIEFS ABOUT MONEY

- Be vigilant about the beliefs to do with money that are lurking in your unconscious mind, and write them down.

- For every limiting belief that comes up, think of and then write down a more empowering replacement belief.

- Think of a sentence that encapsulates your new belief about money and repeat it at least 20 times a day.

- Each morning, while looking in the mirror, hold a conversation with yourself that reinforces your new belief.

- Collect evidence on a daily basis about your new belief, and record it in your journal or notebook.

- Once you have accepted that there is sufficient evidence to support your new belief, choose another limiting belief and repeat the above steps.

Remember, your thoughts and your spoken words create your world. Stay vigilant each day about what you focus on, and what you are creating!

Chapter 3

Loving You,
Loving Money

'Money is not the most important thing in the world.
Love is. Fortunately, I love money.'
– Jackie Mason

This is the part of the book where you choose to welcome money back into your life. If you've been hating money, or resenting it for not showing up in your life, it's not going to feel very welcome in your home.

Your life is all about your relationship with the world around you. When you are in love, the world becomes a brighter place and everyone seems to love you. When you are depressed, it spreads a dark shadow over the brightest of days and everyone appears to be miserable. Can you see that if the very mention of money makes you feel fearful or angry, then you're unlikely to want more of it?

Choose to love money and it will choose to love you. Choose to love and value yourself and others will love and value you.

Choose money as your preferred means of exchange, and you will receive money in exchange for the unique value you give.

Money is simply a way to express your love for yourself and your love for others.

When someone provides something of value to you, you express your gratitude by paying them money. The amount of money you are happy to pay will depend on how much you personally value what they have provided. Whether it's a new TV, a holiday or a cleaning service, we are happy to pay the going rate as a 'thank you' for what we have received. When we are unhappy, though, we express the withdrawal of our love by asking for a refund.

How Much Are You Loving Yourself Right Now?

How much money are you giving yourself? Many people confuse buying treats for themselves, like a new pair of shoes or a 'much needed' holiday, with being loving towards themselves.

Notice what is happening to the money! In buying the shoes or the holiday, the money is going out of your bank account and into the bank account of the shoe or travel company! Yes, you may have a new pair of shoes and you may enjoy a gorgeous holiday, but once the shoes have been worn out and the holiday has come to an end, you will have nothing left to show for your money. Meanwhile, the shoe company and the travel company have your money. In loving your money they will treasure it, and put it in a place where it will earn them more money.

In this example, can you see that the shoe company and the travel company are valuing your money more than you are? It might be time to start taking more care of yourself and your money:

- Decide *now* to show yourself more love.

- Decide *now* to give yourself more money.

- Decide *now* to fall in love with yourself, and to express that love through money.

<u>Money Magnet Mindset Tool: Looking at Your Current Relationship with Money</u>

Ask yourself the following questions and jot down your response:

How much money (love) do you currently have in your life?

....

Do you have any money (love) left for yourself at the end of each month?

....

Who do you value enough to give your money (love) to?

....

Are you giving money (love) away and getting little in return?

....

Are you grateful for the money (love) that you have for yourself?

....

Do you honour and care for the money (yourself) in your life?

....

How often do you have a date with your money (yourself)?

....

How could you love your money (yourself) more?

....

How could you love yourself more by attracting more money?

....

Marks out of ten, how would you score your current relationship with money?

....

Just as you'd develop a loving relationship with someone by spending more time with them, you must choose to spend more quality time with your money. You need to set aside regular dates for just you and your money! Occasionally, you can invite guests who only have the best intentions to help you and your money expand and grow.

The more time you spend with money, the more your relationship will develop, and you will start to attract more of it. This doesn't mean that you become a lonely hoarder. No, just as in every healthy relationship, partners need to have their own lives and passions, independent of each other, and it is important that your life is not all about money.

You are free to choose how you wish to live your life, but by honouring and cherishing money as the most trustworthy partner you can find – one that has no agenda other than the one you choose – you will always feel loved. Money doesn't have a personality. It takes on the personality that you give it. By honouring and cherishing your money, you are honouring and cherishing yourself.

If you treat money with respect, it will earn you more money. For example, when you know that you have enough money put aside for a rainy day, or to be able to take advantage of life's many opportunities when they arise, you will know that you are well looked-after and that you are rich.

A Conversation with Money

So, without further ado, let's start your first conversation with money. This is your first date and so you'll want to find out as much as you can about your money. You know that the likelihood is that the more you learn about you and your relationship with money, the more you are going to learn about yourself!

How much do you value your money? If you want to have more money, you need to value the money you do have. In my experience, there are two possible reasons why you might not be earning more money:

1. You are not really interested in money (you only think you are!).

2. You are not 'playing a big enough game' in life.

One way to find out how much you value money is to look at the amount of time you devote to it. If you take up a new hobby, you find the hours in your day to accommodate your new passion. If you fall in love, you make time to see that person, however busy you are!

We all have a hierarchy of values and we view the world through those values.

If you don't place money or being wealthy on your list of top values, you could be sitting on a gold mine and just not see it!

Money Magnet Mindset Tool: Making Time for Your Money

How much time do you set aside for managing your money, and for learning more about money? The way you allocate your time during a typical week can give you a good idea of your values and priorities. For example, if you spend three hours a week at the gym but only 30 minutes a week on your accounts, then money may be less important to you than health and fitness.

Complete the following table to find out how you currently allocate your time.

Activity	Hours Spent On it Per Week
Family	
Children	
Career (earning money)	
Home	
Holidays/leisure	
Personal education	
Watching TV	

What percentage of your time do you currently spend earning and managing your money?

....

How could you increase the amount of time you spend with your money?

....

....

What might you have to give up in order to spend more time with your money?
(For example: 'One hour of TV per night.')

....

....

If you love your life but are always finding yourself short of money, it's time to allocate more time to do your accounts, research investments, boost your income and track your financial performance. If you want more money, the very first thing you need to do is look at how much time you currently devote to money. By taking more time out to manage and enhance your financial situation, you will be sending out the appropriate energetic message that you are serious about wanting more money.

Managing What Comes In and What Goes Out!

So, let's look at how interested you really are in manifesting more money. If you are going to manifest more money, you need to look at how much money you currently have. Yes, you can ask for £1million, but unless you get down and dirty with your money, it will still occur as something that has nothing to do with you.

If you want a relationship with someone, you need to spend time with them and get up close to them. It's the same if you want to have a sweeter relationship with money, and if you want to see more of it! Asking for £1million is like asking for a date with George Clooney – unless you already know George quite well, the odds of that date happening are probably about one in a million!

Now is the time to choose to get interested in money and how it shows up in your life! Understanding *exactly* how much money you have right now will give you a certain peace of mind and the power to improve your finances.

Do you look at your finances in the way that you watch a horror film: with your hands over your eyes, always imagining things to be far worse than they usually are? Remember, you have the inner resources to resolve any situation, but if you don't understand the full extent of the problem, your brain can't get started on finding a solution!

Your first important step is to create a very simple income and expenditure chart. I recommend that you update this every month so you feel on top of the flow of money in your life and can track any changes as they happen. Reviewing your monthly cashflow will allow you to avoid that panicky feeling you get when an unexpected bill comes in, and you will start to feel more self-confident and in control of your life. You will become the Master of your Money, rather than the victim of never having enough of it!

Money Magnet Mindset Tool: Creating an Income and Expenditure Chart

It's a good idea to allocate a few hours to creating a chart like the one below. Be prepared to get out all your bills and bank statements so you have accurate figures to hand. Start to get curious about how you earn, invest and spend your money.

Income	Monthly Value (£)
Net salary	
State benefits	
Interest on investments/savings	
Rental income	
Other income (e.g. online sales, babysitting, car boot sales, etc)	
Total income (1)	

Fixed Expenditure	Monthly Value (£)
Mortgage/rent	
Loan repayments	
Credit card repayments	
Water/gas/electricity	
Telephone/mobile/internet	
Council tax	
Home and contents insurance	
Life/health insurance	
Car insurance	
Travel insurance	
Pet insurance	
TV licence/rental/Cable/Sky TV	
Child-minding/school fees	
Pension contributions	
Personal savings and investments	
Gym membership/personal trainer	
Personal coach /mentor	
Club/online memberships	
Subscriptions (e.g. charity)	
Total fixed expenditure (2)	

Variable Expenditure	Monthly Value (£)
Food and drink	
Household/toiletries	
Cosmetics/hair and beauty treatments	
Clothes and shoes	
Eating and drinking out/ entertainment	
Music/films	
Hobbies/sports	
Children's pocket money	
Treatments/therapies	
Lunch at work/when travelling	
Travel costs (train, tube, taxi)	
Petrol	
Cleaning (car, house, windows)	
Dry cleaning/shoe repair	
Bank charges	
Unallocated cash spending	
Other	
Total variable expenditure (3)	

Occasional Expenditure	Monthly Value (£)
Holidays/weekends away	
Gifts and cards/Christmas	
One-off items (e.g. new phone/TV)	
Home improvements	
Car tax/MOT/repairs /service	
Dental/eye care	
Child/school expenses	
Luxury therapies/treatments	
Other	
Total occasional expenditure (4)	

Totals	Monthly Value (£)
Total Income (1)	
Total fixed expenditure (2)	
Total variable expenditure (3)	
Total occasional expenditure (4)	
Total available to you: **(1) minus (2), (3) and (4)**	

▓ Case Study: Managing Your Way Out of Debt

I first met Suzanne at a Money Magnet workshop in Birmingham. She was a project manager who had amassed more than £28,000 of debt. She realized that she had to take action, and to change her habits around money. By compiling her own spreadsheet of monthly incomings and outgoings like the one above, Suzanne was able to see, at any time during any month, *exactly* how much money she had in her accounts.

You could say that Suzanne's relationship with money shifted from one of ignorance and abuse to one of love and passion! Once she became a lover and a master of her money, she was able to put together a workable plan that cleared her total debt within two years. The best bit was, she was still able to enjoy her life, as long as she kept to the plan.

Money Magnet Mindset Tool: Mastering Your Money

Start now to take control of *your* money by creating a simple Excel spreadsheet for your monthly income and expenditure.

Step 1: Reproduce the chart above as an Excel spreadsheet, customizing it to your own needs.

Step 2: Align the expenditure categories down the left-hand side and the months of the year across the top.

Step 3: Use the AutoSUM function in Excel to calculate your totals for each category and each month.

You may be shocked to see how much per year you are spending on some items. For example, I realized recently that I was spending huge amounts on rail travel. However, once I saw how much it added up to in a year, I resolved to pay less for it. Now I plan and book my journeys in advance, and as a result I have reduced the total expenditure to a third of what I was paying before. That means a lot more money is available for me!

Your spreadsheet will give you a clear picture of your relationship with money, and most importantly, how much money you are paying yourself! Have a play to see what difference it would make each month if you were to spend less in some areas. How can you tweak your spreadsheet to make more money for you? Hey, you might even start to look forward to your dates with your Excel spreadsheet! If you are like me and you've always dreaded doing the detail, this is a tool that can help you view doing your accounts as a fun and creative exercise. I promise you that the more you focus on your money, and specifically on increasing the amount of money you have, the more you will attract it!

One of the best ways to earn money is by being an entrepreneur, but you do need to understand how to do a cashflow forecast, and to read a profit and loss sheet. Even if you are just looking to save and invest wisely, you need to keep an eye on interest rates, as things are changing all the time. As the old saying goes: 'the devil is in the detail'!

Fatima proudly announced to me that all her credit card debt was at either 0% or 3.74% interest per annum. She had more than £36,000 of debt, and when we double-checked her accounts we found that the 0% interest rate had expired on one of her cards and she was now paying 19.9% on more than £10,000 of debt. To say that this got her focused would be an understatement! If she had been paying attention to the detail, she would have had a debt repayment plan in place, and would have known the expiry date for the 0% interest rate *and* what she was going to do about it – in advance!

Most of the stress around money comes from people turning a blind eye. The funny thing is, that once you really start to take an interest in your money, you will either find that you have more than you thought you had, or you will start to attract more of it.

> *You attract more of what you focus on, so now is the time to get interested in your money!*

If you haven't yet created your own Income and Expenditure spreadsheet, do it now! You will feel so good once it is completed, and you will know where you are with your money. It will be like your very first kiss with a new date!

■ Case Study: Focus on Your Cashflow and Watch the Cash Flow in!

I received the following letter from Sue Hills, who is managing director of a branch of home care provider Caremark:

'Shortly after reading *How to Become a Money Magnet* I began to look at my cashflow situation in a different way. Rather than seeing it as doom and gloom, I now looked at it as an opportunity to get a grip on my finances and was grateful that it had happened before it was too late. I then did a new cashflow and profit and loss forecast, and was very excited and optimistic when I saw that, provided I remained within budget, it looked very positive.

'Almost immediately, money started flowing into my account, from both expected and unexpected sources. For example, some money came in which I had previously written off as bad debt, and monies that I did not expect until later also came in to relieve the cashflow situation. I also received an inspiration to combine my two offices into one, which was something that I had never thought of before, again saving me both money and time.

'The learning I have taken from this is to understand that I do create my own reality – both positively and negatively – and the evidence is all around me if I look for it!'

Pay Yourself First

Now that you're starting to value your relationship with money, you need to know the most basic rule of wealth accumulation. This rule is: *always pay yourself first*. Now this doesn't mean splashing out on a new TV, or treating yourself to a weekend away, no matter how good it may feel. When you do that you are giving your hard-earned cash to the retailer or to the travel agent.

Paying yourself first means putting aside a minimum of 10% of your earnings to save and invest in you having a secure financial future. Sounds boring? Just imagine if you had savings right now of, say, £700,000, which were generating a monthly income for you of £3,000 – how boring does that sound? I know one entrepreneur who puts aside 50% of his earnings and encourages his children to do the same. It certainly makes sense for a business owner to do this, even if it is just to know that they have money put aside to pay all taxes or fees due.

Just think of the peace of mind you will have in knowing that someone is taking care of you, and that you have some money put aside for emergencies. I tell you, it will make it a lot easier to think happy thoughts about money than if you are always wondering where the next penny is coming from, or living in fear that your main source of income will be taken away from you, or that your business may go under when you receive the tax bill.

Money Magnet Mindset Tool: Paying Yourself First

Automatically transfer between 10 and 50% of your earnings to at least one savings account each month.

If you are worried about bills, you will have a fearful and needy Money Mindset, and it goes almost without saying that this is not what will make you a Money Magnet! Remember, you attract more of what you focus on. Focus on the bills and the debt and they will increase.

> *Focus on how much you are saving each month, or how you can make more profit by giving more value, and you will attract more profit and be more valued by your customers!*

Makes sense doesn't it? However, it's not always that easy to do when you are worried about where the next penny is coming from.

Money Magnet Mindset Tool: Creating 'Worry Time'

This tool comes from Dr Jen Nash, who is a clinical psychologist and an official Money Magnet.

If money worries are starting to get on top of you, and invading your thoughts, set a daily 'worry time'. You can make this as long as you like: 15 minutes, 30 minutes, or even an hour. Try to have your 'worry time' at the same time each day, though.

During your scheduled 'worry time', you must concentrate fully on your money worries. Write them all down and focus on them. The chances are that you won't need the full allocation of time!

What we are doing here is training your brain to recognize that it will always have a daily time to worry, and so it needn't worry for the rest of the day. It's worth persisting with this exercise and maybe using an alarm to signify the end of the worry time. If you can train your brain to worry for a strictly limited time each day, imagine how gorgeous the rest of your day will be, and what a fantastic reality you will then create from those happy, worry-free thoughts!

Banish Your Money Worries

If you have a big bill to pay that you *can't* pay, or another big concern about your money, it is *very important* that you do the following:

- Look the issue square in the face and establish the facts and any possible solutions – avoid drama or an emotional reaction. An unpaid bill is just an unpaid bill. It doesn't mean anything about you as a person. It just means that you haven't paid a bill and now you need to pay it.

- Communicate with all parties involved, even if it is just to acknowledge their bill and to let them know when you will next be in contact. Lack of communication is the one thing most likely to worsen the situation, so keep talking to your suppliers and stay clear and positive. No whingeing, or 'poor me' outbursts – they won't help anyone, least of all you!

- Take action to resolve the issue. Remember, nearly everything in life is negotiable! If you can't settle the bill all at once, agree a payment schedule, or request an interest holiday. Taking action will clear your mind and immediately help you to feel better about yourself... and when you feel better about yourself you're more likely to attract more opportunities to make money!

A Conversation with Debt

Look at the money facts. For example, if you are worried about your credit card debt, face up to it. Take out your credit card statements and create an Excel spreadsheet of what you owe and to whom, and place the debts in order of highest penalty or interest rate first. For example, if you are behind on your mortgage, keeping a roof over your head is likely to be your top priority, particularly if you have a family.

Get really interested in your debt, and you will start to get creative. By just facing up to it, you will feel better and it will feel less like a scary monster hiding in the cupboard. Similarly, if you run a business, keep an eye on your cashflow situation and then start to have fun finding new ways to make more profit – either by simple economies or by creating more value.

If you look at any successful entrepreneur, you will most likely observe someone who is always having ideas about how to make more money. In almost every situation, they will see the money-making opportunity. It is fun to spot the opportunities in life, and to play a game of 'How can I make money here?'

Only when you have a clear idea about how much money you have coming in and going out each month will you be in a position to make a powerful difference to your finances. Only when you are 'in the conversation' with money will your thoughts be ones that attract opportunities to earn more of it. This is about managing your thoughts so they become aligned to those of a Money Magnet.

Janet was terribly worried about the amount of debt she was in. Then she worried about the negative thoughts she was having about her debt. *These are not the thoughts of a Money Magnet*, she thought, *but I need to worry about the debt. Not to do so would mean that I am being irresponsible!* The problem was, this type of thinking was not going to get her out of the situation!

I recommended that Janet get back into a healthy Money Magnet Mindset by using the technique below, which was inspired by Michael Neill's book *You Can Have What You Want,* and by The Sedona Method. It really works – even when you are facing the biggest money issues. If you wake up in the morning feeling fearful and worried about your money, put a bookmark in this page and use this tool regularly until it starts to occur to you naturally. It's the Money Magnet equivalent of an anti-depressant – and far healthier for you in my opinion!

Money Magnet Mindset Tool: Loving the Monster!

Step 1: Think of your biggest, scariest issue regarding money right now.

Step 2: Feel the fear and allow the panic to start to set in.

Step 3: Now make *a conscious choice to love the problem you have.*

Step 4: Choose to love your debt, your fears, and your worries about not having enough money.

As soon as you complete these steps, the metaphorical cloud will lift, I promise.

Weird as it sounds, this is a wonderful technique for letting go of your negative mindset around money. The more you embrace what you have been running from, the less fearful it appears. It may seem strange at first, but give it a go right now.

Think of your biggest money problem, choose to love it just as it is and you may even find that you burst into laughter! What once seemed so scary and stressful has now been released, leaving you in a much more powerful place to deal with the solution. Remember, you are not likely to attract more money if you are coming from a fearful, negative mindset.

> *Money is your bedfellow in life and it's always a good idea to love who you're sleeping with! Declare now that you are going to fall in love with your money from now on, and allow money to fall in love with you!*

Congratulations on completing this chapter, and for taking the time to get 'under the sheets' with your finances!

■ Case Study: Overcoming a Fear of Money

Jeannie was a marketing manager in her fifties who had become scared of money while renovating her home. As the bills came in through her letterbox, she would collect the envelopes and walk over to the table, where she would carefully place them on top of a pile of other unopened bills. The pile was now considerably high.

'How do you know how much the bill is if you don't open the envelope?' I asked her. *'Oh,'* she said, *'I have a vague idea!'* The problem was that, until her mind knew *exactly* what monies had to be paid, it would be left wondering just how much money she needed to find to pay the bill. Until her mind knew how much money needed to be paid, it couldn't possibly be sure that the resources were there to pay it.

Can you see how, by avoiding opening her bills, Jeannie was actually *increasing* the amount of fear and uncertainty she had around money? Money, in the form of unpaid and unopened bills, now had a grasp on her and until she faced the reality, she would remain a victim of those bills and demands for money. When she understood this, she started opening her bills. The fear evaporated and each month she found it actually pretty easy to pay all her bills.

MONEY MAGNET MINDSET HABITS: START A LOVE AFFAIR WITH MONEY

- Open your bills enthusiastically!

- Schedule a regular time each month to review your Income and Expenditure spreadsheet.

- Keep looking (daily!) at how you can increase the money available to you.

- Have a manageable payment plan to cover large bills and debts.

- Pay off the debts with the highest interest rate first.

- Use direct debits to keep all essential payments up to date.

- Ensure that you have an emergency cash fund to cover 3–6 months' expenditure.

- Nurture yourself and your money by saving regularly and investing wisely.

- Set up savings accounts for holidays, savings, investments, charities, your personal development, and so on.

- Set up monthly direct debits from your current account into your savings accounts.

- Contact your suppliers and ask for their best deal.

- Speak lovingly of your relationship with money.

- Get a Lasting Power of Attorney drawn up with a solicitor to manage your accounts should you become incapable of doing so.

- Make a will.

- Get interested in money: read the financial papers, watch TV programmes on money, and so on.

- Have fun with your money!

- Enjoy finding new and creative ways to have more money!

Remember, the more you focus on something, the more of it you will attract! Acknowledge your new appreciation of money and yourself!

Chapter 4

Choose to Have More Money

'None of us will ever accomplish anything excellent
or commanding except when he listens to this whisper
which is heard by him alone.'
– Thomas Carlyle

So, you now understand that you are the creator of your life, and responsible for the amount of money that shows up in it. You have uncovered the core limiting beliefs that were cluttering up your creative channels, and you have embraced your relationship with money. You are now free to choose what you want in your life – including how much money you would like to receive.

How exciting is that?

So many people tell me that they want to have more money, but when I ask them, 'How much, and by when?' they are dumbfounded. If you cannot decide what it is that you want, you will never be able to achieve it. It's the obvious first step.

Money Magnet Mindset Tool: Choosing the Life and the Money That You Really Want

Take a moment to consider the questions below and to write down your response. Don't judge your answers, and don't doubt them. Accept the first answer that comes to you for each question.

What do you want most in life?
(For example: 'I want to be happy and loved.')

....

....

Exactly how much money do you want?
(For example: 'I want £1million.')

....

When do you want to have this money?
(For example: 'I want it by the last day of this year.'

....

Until you have the answers to these three very simple questions, you cannot progress to the next stages in this book. I recommend that you start each year by asking yourself these questions. You can also use this technique on a daily basis.

For question two, did you pick a wildly unrealistic sum, or did you behave cautiously when choosing your money? Did you put down a conservative figure based on what you thought you could achieve?

*Start to get interested in what **you** really want, regardless of what others around you may wish for you, what you think is socially acceptable, or what you think might be possible.*

I'd like you now to let go of what you *know* you can achieve and look just a little beyond to what you think could be possible for you if you just dare yourself to dream it. If you want to have more money than you have now, I suggest you choose a figure that is more than you've previously thought would be possible for you. Don't choose a totally impossible figure, though – like £100million in one month – as that may well be a way of unconsciously setting yourself up for failure.

As soon as Elaine was introduced to me she said, *'I know who you are. We are looking to find £1million within three months – can you help us?'* That was a clear intention and a powerful public declaration. Elaine didn't achieve £1million in three months, but she did achieve £400,000 in four months. Would she have achieved that amount – which is still spectacular within such a short amount of time – if she hadn't been so clear and purposeful? I doubt it. The interesting thing was that by the end of the year, Elaine had achieved a business delivering an annual turnover of £1.1million!

Money Magnet Mindset Tool: Embracing Your Desires

Keep a journal and start up a conversation between yourself and another version of yourself about what you want from your life.

Keep asking yourself what you really want, and pay attention to the answers!

Make a list of your top priorities and values in life.

Then make sure that you acknowledge yourself every time you make a choice in your day that honours what you do want!

Get What You Do Want by Saying 'No' to What You Don't Want

When you start getting clear on what you do want, it'll be easier to see what you don't want. For most people, it's easier to say 'yes' than 'no'. The child in us wants to say 'yes' to everything, no matter what the consequences may be. The word 'no' may bring back childhood memories of an adult telling you that you couldn't have what you wanted because it was not good for you. Well, it's time for *you* to become the adult now.

Only you can be responsible for your life and the choices you make within it. It's time for you to say 'no' to the things you don't want, and in so doing, you will create the life that you do want! Whenever you say 'no' to something you don't want – whether it's a chocolate, another business opportunity or a romantic date – it is a declaration of what you are really committed to having in your life: a healthy, slim body, your *own* business achieving its goals, or being with a certain person.

It is the big choices we make that set our direction. It is the smallest choices we make that get us to the destination.

Recently, I was following a strict detox regime and no solid food had passed my lips for seven days. While sitting alone in my lounge, I found a wrapped chocolate that my god-daughter had given me the previous week. I picked it up and considered my thoughts on the situation. 'I could just pop this into my mouth and no one would know', I thought. 'It's only small; it won't do any harm.' But inside I knew that it was not what I was committed to, and the moment that I chose *not* to eat that chocolate was the moment that I knew I really was committed to valuing myself and my choices. In that one choice I increased my perceived value and enhanced my personal self-esteem. Multiply that moment 100 times, and you can see how you can substantially increase your value through the simple choices that you make every day.

If you want to increase the amount of money you have, you will do so in the choices you make every day.

Recently, my good friend Jacqui popped in for a chat. She shared how delighted she was to have treated herself to a brand new red poncho. She told me how she had seen the poncho in the shop the previous week, but hadn't wanted to part with the amount of money they were asking for it.

Instead of reaching for the plastic and indulging her impulsive desire for the top, she honoured her financial commitments for that month and turned her back on it. In saying 'no' in that moment, she demonstrated a higher value for herself and her word than she had for the item of clothing or the pleasure of wearing it. She demonstrated how much she valued her money and her right to have more money.

Jacqui's delight that evening was down to the fact that she had met her financial commitments, had some money left over to spend, and, on passing by the shop, she noticed that the poncho had been reduced to half price! It was the last one left in the shop and she bought it! Now that's what I call a win-win situation.

The inner peace and contentment achieved in this example were so much more valuable than the rush of excitement you'll get from making unplanned, impulsive purchases that weigh on your mind, and on your balance sheet, for a good while afterwards, and leave you ultimately with less money. If you seriously want to have more money, you need to demonstrate that desire in your daily choices. In doing so, you start to retrain your unconscious mind to become a Money Magnet!

Examine the Choices You Make in Your Life

What messages are you currently sending to your unconscious mind? If, for example, you say 'no' to business networking events after 6 p.m., you may be more committed to watching TV or spending time with your family in the evenings. There is nothing necessarily wrong with this, but if you want to promote your business, or find new clients, this is not what you are acting out in the choice you've made. Your choices need to be consistent with your values and what you want from your life.

Similarly, if you are saying that you are committed to becoming a Money Magnet, but you would rather go for a drink with friends than call the last potential customer on your list, then you may find that your commitment is more to having fun or being liked than it is to earning money!

Now, clearly we all want to have it all. I'm certainly not suggesting that you should forego all the fun in your life to have more money. The point is that your actions need to be aligned with what you are choosing for yourself, every day. Start to become more conscious of the daily choices you make, and you will realize what is really most important to you. You may even find that you haven't been wanting more money after all!

Money Magnet Mindset Tool: Aligning Your Actions With What You Want

Write the question below on a piece of card, display it in a prominent place, and keep asking yourself it.

'How are my actions aligned to having more money?'

When you realize that you haven't been choosing to have more money, only then will you start to consciously choose whether you do now want more money or not!

Remember, money will buy you more time with your family and friends, but you may need to give up some of that time *now* in order to make it happen later. My solution is to work with my family and friends, and to choose to love my work!

Choice vs Need

If you are focused on what you *need* to have in order to be happy, you won't be able to be happy until you get it. We have all met those needy people. You want to run away from them, don't you? Can you see how this sort of focus is repellent to others, and to the energy of money?

If you are coming from a place of 'What's in it for me?' you will assume that everyone else is coming from that place and you will often feel used. You will feel that you are always searching for the answers from other people, rather than listening to your own inner voice. It can be exhausting! Choose now to honour the wisdom within you, and to make your own choices.

As you saw in the last chapter, it is important to be aware of your current financial situation; you need to get real about it and to look at the impact if you continue to live in your current relationship with money. If a friend was in an abusive relationship, you would want to wake her up to the reality of what was happening. It is the same scenario if you have an abusive relationship with money. Facing up to what's really happening is taking responsibility for your life, and you are not being needy when you take care of your own needs.

Face Up to Your Biggest Nightmare

Many people's worst nightmare would be bankruptcy. But it is not bankruptcy itself that destroys a person's sense of worth.

I know many people who have been through the needle of bankruptcy and come out the better for it. They have stopped pushing so hard to get what they want. They have become more compassionate, to themselves and to others, and they have learnt that their possessions, or lack of them, are not what defines them.

They have learnt to listen to their inner voice and to honour what is important to them. They can now make powerful choices, and many of them go on to attract much more money than they had attracted in the past! They have learnt the impact of not being responsible, and now choose to become responsible for their lives.

> *'The outer passes away; the innermost is the same*
> *yesterday, today and forever.'*
> – **Thomas Carlyle**

Choose a Positive Mindset

Recently I received a call from a colleague who had just been made bankrupt after years of fighting to survive and pay back his debts. It hadn't been his choice to go bankrupt. However, instead of hearing a sob story, I heard him talk of how he was wealthier now, and how he was no longer a magnet for debt. He had received incredible support and love from friends, and it had freed him up to do what he wanted to do.

Now, I am not for one second advocating that you choose to go bankrupt. There are lots of yucky downsides to it – like losing your bank accounts, your website and your company director status. What I do want to point out though is that, even in the most dire circumstances, it is your mindset that ultimately determines the quality of your life. Rather than succumb to the 'poor me' syndrome, this guy had mastered a magnificently wealthy mindset and he already has a plan of how he'll achieve £1million in the next year! With that new mindset, I have no doubt that he will, too!

What defines you is what you think about yourself. The person who ultimately defines your value is you (more on this in Part 3), and you define your value in the choices you make every day.

Money Magnet Mindset Tool: How Often do You Choose More Money?

Become aware of all the times when you are conscious of choosing to have less money. Ask yourself the following:

Do you charge less than the going rate because you want someone to like you?

Do you pay more than your share on a night out just to keep everyone happy?

Would you rather pay more than face a conversation about money?

Do you pay more for something because you can't be bothered to shop around?

Start noting down in your journal or notebook the exact moments when you now consciously choose to have more money for yourself.

Are You Really Committed to Having More Money?

You may be starting to realize why you don't have the money that you say you want – you haven't been choosing it on a day-to-day basis. You may have been *saying* that you want to have more money, but that's not the same as actively *choosing* to have more money. If you don't have much money now, that's a pretty good clue that you haven't really been committed to having more money. However, you have chosen to read this book, so I invite you to be open to the idea that you *do* actually want to have more money, at least on some level!

If you have completed all the exercises in this book so far, then I congratulate you. In making that choice to do the work, you have shifted yourself into the space of being someone who is committed to becoming a Money Magnet! It is in honouring that commitment to yourself on a daily basis, and in defiance of the little voice in you that may be protesting, that you will achieve all your financial dreams. Yes, you can have all the money that you've ever wanted.

> *Money doesn't discriminate – it comes to those who choose it.*

A Money Magnet Mindset is created in every choice you make that is aligned with being a Money Magnet. If you *haven't* yet done the exercises in the book, and you are starting to think that 'there are more important things in life than money', you are right, and money is not at the top of your priorities right now. Yes, of course you might like to have more money, but you are just not fully committed to the idea. You don't want to give up anything, do anything that feels uncomfortable or inconvenient, or make any sacrifices just now. Maybe it all feels a little too much like hard work? That's okay. It's just that you haven't yet found your big reason to choose money.

You need to have a really good reason why you want more money if you are to change the habits that are aligned with you having less money. If you don't have a big enough *why* to choose money, then it will continue to elude you. You will keep doing what you've always done. If you read the books on becoming wealthy but never do anything different, you will remain someone who reads books on money and never does anything different.

Having a big reason to want more will push you into doing something different. If, for example, you want £1million by the end of this year so you can do what you've always wanted to do – whether it's building an orphanage, ensuring your future financial security or creating a property portfolio – it just has to be a good enough reason for you. Bear in mind, though, that to *receive* an extra £1million in just one year you'll need to find a way of *offering* £1million-worth of extra value to others! You need to become someone who is worthy of receiving £1million.

Money Magnet Miracle

Aggy had a massive reason 'why' she should have more money. She had created a home-based business called Aggy's Sauces of Hope as a way of providing money for children in Zambia whose lives have been affected by AIDS.

A small black woman with an infectious laugh and a fantastically positive and uplifting viewpoint on life, Aggy spoke out

passionately whenever she could to promote her business. She did whatever she could to make it work, and she never stopped trying and investing in herself and her business. Every choice she made in life was aligned with attracting more money for her business.

Aggy chose to come on a Money Magnet workshop and a couple of months after it, she attracted her pick of no fewer than five Angel Investors, all looking to put £50,000 into her business! In fact, by the time this book is published, I'm expecting to see Aggy's sauces on my local supermarket shelf (check her out at www.aggyssauces.com).

Aggy's massive reason 'why' was the thing that kept her committed to her financial targets and that drove her forward to make the right choices, even when she couldn't see where the money was going to come from.

What is Your Reason 'Why'?

Your reason 'why' doesn't have to be as big and charitable as Aggy's. It could be that you want to have more money so that you can feel better about yourself, or so that you can provide a secure future for yourself and your family. It could be that you want to prove to someone, even yourself, that you can do it.

It could even be out of revenge! The great motivational speaker Jim Rohn tells how he was once inspired to get more money just so he could get back at a car salesman who'd been rude to him years earlier. Jim entered the car showroom to settle the final balance due on his car. He walked into the centre of the room, where the salesman was sitting, carrying a briefcase full of banknotes in the smallest denomination. Without a

word, he then ceremoniously tipped all the banknotes over the salesman's head before leaving the showroom!

Money Magnet Mindset Tool: Why More Money?

Write down your response to the following questions:

What is *one* driving force behind your desire for money?

....

....

How will you feel once you have enough money?
(For example: 'At peace', or 'confident'.)

....

What choices become available to you when you have more money?
(For example: 'I could buy a sports car.')

....

What difference could you make in the world with an abundant flow of money?

....

....

How much more money would you need in order to live the life of your dreams?

....

It is a good idea to consider your core values when answering these questions. Ask yourself what is really important to you, as opposed to what you think others would approve of. I once

thought that my biggest drive was to make a difference to others and to global poverty, and then I realized that I was doing that already! I looked again and realized that my biggest drive was actually to have more fun in my life, and to enjoy laughing as much as possible with other people. Watch out for me on your nearest stand-up comedy circuit!

■ *Case Study: Big Dreams Lead to Big Money*

Elaine had a big reason why she wanted £1million. She is the proud custodian of The Monastery in Manchester – a spiritual centre open to all religions – and she is committed to her vision of a united world. To find out more about this amazing place, visit www.themonastery.co.uk.

Both Aggy and Elaine were driven by a desire to provide money for others, which is wonderful and it works for them. However, don't fall into the trap of providing for others at the exclusion of providing for yourself. That will only lead to bitterness and resentment.

When the great US steel magnate Andrew Carnegie passed away, they found a note he had written about what he had wanted from his life. In it, he said that he wanted to spend the first half of his life accumulating as much wealth as possible, and the second half getting rid of it as fast as possible. Carnegie accumulated $450million and then proceeded to spend it all in the second half of his life. A modern-day equivalent of this would be Bill Gates and his wife Melinda, and their philanthropic work.

It's Crucial to Focus on Money if You Want to Have More of it

The money you have is a reflection of how much you value yourself. Ask yourself:

- Are you not worth having the life of your dreams?

- Are your skills and gifts not worth someone paying you handsomely for them?

- Have you not spent a lifetime creating the unique person of value that you are?

It is time for you to receive your worthy reward.

Some people suggest that you can translate the money you want into your individual vision of wealth. For example, instead of thinking of the $5million you'd need to buy a yacht, you simply think of experiencing sailing on that yacht. That's fine, but in my experience you will attract a wonderful sailing opportunity but you will still have exactly the same amount of money in your bank account.

You need to be very clear about what you want. While a sailing holiday would be fabulous, it might be good to have some savings in your bank account, or to have the security of your own home sorted first. Otherwise, you'll return from the sailing holiday to face the problems that you had before you went away.

Living a life of fun and luxury is fabulous! Living a life where you know you have taken care of your financial security is calm and comforting. Living a life where you have both is simply heaven!

It's Time for You to Choose Money!

Have you noticed how wealthy people always look after the pennies? They know that every penny saved and earned increases their personal value. They achieve a boost to their self-esteem when they know they have achieved a significant sum of money for themselves as a direct result of their endeavours.

Money is the measure of value, and not to value money is to effectively opt out of society. The only other reason why you might think you do not want money is because you believe there is something bad about wanting money and you want to be seen as a good person. Can you see that you already are a good person, and having more money will not make you bad or good, unless that is what you choose to believe?

*If you are really clear that money is not important to you, and that you have no desire to be wealthy, then I suggest that you honour your personal choice, close this book now, and donate it to someone who **does** want more money in their life!*

If you are still reading, then I will assume that you have answered the questions above for yourself, done the exercises so far in this book, and that you are committed and ready to welcome more money into your life. Congratulations!!

If I asked you: *'How much money do you want, and by when?'* you will now have a clear answer. And now that you are focused on having an exact amount of money by a certain time, you'll want to maintain and master that focus on a daily basis so you cannot fail to achieve your desired results.

Money Magnet Mindset Tool: Staying Focused on Your Desired Financial Outcome

Write down again your financial goal, and the date by which you will achieve it. (Note: this should be the same figure that you recorded earlier in this chapter.)

Amount ....

Date...

During Money Magnet workshops, I often witness declarations for more money that are then forgotten within a matter of months. Life kicks in, the usual complaints come too easily to a person's lips, and before they know it, any idea of a breakthrough around money seems like a distant memory.

Staying Focused on What You Want

So, how do you maintain your focus on what you want, especially when the evidence around you is telling you that you can't have it?

If you have always wanted a certain amount of money, say £50,000 a year, and now you choose to have £500,000, you are going to have to train your mind to discard the old thoughts and stay focused on the new thoughts. The good news is that it is entirely possible to retrain your thoughts. The bad news is that it may require some discipline.

We have already looked at how important it is to recognize unconscious limiting beliefs so you can choose to let them go. The problem is, we are creatures of habit, so your mind will not always let go of entrenched belief systems without a bit of a fight. Without effort, the mind will slip back into its default belief system, and it may require real conscious effort, at least for a while, to retrain it and to choose more positive thoughts.

Let me share an example with you. Imagine that I don't believe anyone will buy my book. I am convinced that it's stupid to even be writing the book, since I know that the publisher won't like it, and that no one will buy it. I then recognize that this belief is in place so I don't have to put myself on the line and risk failure.

The benefit of this belief is that I am 'covered' if no one likes my book; I cannot fail because I will have been right about it. And, like most people, I like to be right about what I believe! Now, clearly this is not a very good belief system to have in place if you are writing a book, least of all a book that is capable of changing people's lives for the better! But, now that I've recognized this belief, I can choose a more empowering one. I can choose instead to focus on the many people who will be helped by my book. I can choose to focus on the many people who bought my first book, or on the faith that my publisher has in me.

I can choose to enjoy writing the book and I can start to visualize it becoming a worldwide success. It is a book that changes lives, and inspires people to be all they can be. It is a book that will be recommended by one friend to another as people strive to achieve financial and personal success. Now all this feels great, and I am inspired to continue writing for hours!

But when I wake up the next morning, the old feelings return. I say to myself: 'What's the point? It will never get finished. It's no good!' It is at that very point that I have the opportunity to master my thought patterns, rather than becoming a victim of them. Do not wait for the thoughts to go away before you start to feel inspired. As soon as you recognize the intrusion of self-limiting thoughts, it is *your* job, and no one else's, to change your mind!

At first this may seem impossible, but trust me, with practice it becomes easier and easier. You will start to see that the real you is not the product of your thoughts and feelings; the real you can be, do, or have anything you wish – once you are no longer a slave to your default settings! The trick is to stay vigilant, be inspired, and keep focused on what you want!

Transformation Comes with Consistently Making New Choices

Another example would be if I were committed to losing weight. The first step would be to become conscious of what and how I am eating, because it is only when I become conscious of my behaviour and thoughts that I can consciously choose to change them in the moment.

In her book *Eating Less,* Gillian Riley recommends that you decide in advance when you are next going to eat. It doesn't matter if it will be in ten minutes or in ten hours, it is simply a technique to make you conscious of when you are eating.

I remember celebrating my birthday a few years back and, after having lunch with my mother, I consciously chose that I would eat next at 6 p.m. We returned to my home and I put on the kettle to make us afternoon tea. On the counter was a small birthday cake that my mother had bought for me, and I suggested that we eat some with our tea. It was 5 p.m. and I realized then that I was thinking about eating before I had actually planned to eat. In other words, I wasn't honouring my commitment to myself. Now conscious of an unconscious choice, I asked myself why I wanted to eat cake at that moment.

The response I received was enlightening: I wanted to eat the cake because:

1. Cake is meant to be eaten with a cup of tea.

2. It was tea time.

3. It was a birthday cake, so it was meant to be eaten on a birthday.

4. Birthdays are to be celebrated with the eating of cake.

5. It is polite to share the gift of cake with the person who has given you the gift.

The one good reason for eating something would be because I was hungry, and yet this reason didn't feature anywhere on my list! And let me be clear, I was not about to just eat the cake. I was going to scoff down every last crumb, whether I was hungry or not!!

It had absolutely nothing to do with being hungry, or consciously wanting to eat cake! The moment I realized this, I also realized that I'd never particularly liked cake, and I was now only eating it to please my mother – no doubt a thought pattern installed after years of my mother asking me to finish my plate as a young child!

After one tiny nibble of the cake, my mother and I actually decided that it looked better than it tasted, and we ate no more of it. I disposed of the cake shortly afterwards, and in doing so, broke with another ingrained belief that you should never throw food away! I had been able to recognize an unconscious thought, to then make a conscious choice, and in doing so, to start transforming a lifetime of unconscious eating patterns.

You can apply the same technique to your money habits. If, by doing your accounts, you have already uncovered that you spend more than you earn, or that you'd like to save more and spend less, why not apply the technique below to find out where you are unconsciously giving money away.

Money Magnet Mindset Tool: Planning Your Daily Spending

Step 1: Create a money diary to record your planned daily purchases.

Step 2: To become more conscious of your money habits, choose in advance how much money you are going to spend each day.

Step 3: Decide in advance whether you're going to buy that coffee on the way to work, and whether you'll buy a muffin to go with it.

You can choose to spend as much as you like for the purposes of this exercise, as long as that amount is recorded in advance of spending the money. Start to notice when and why you overspend.

A simple example of this exercise would be to take a list with you when you go supermarket shopping and notice when you are led astray from it. Which items are irresistible to you? How do you justify buying them when you had not consciously chosen them in the first place? What is the unconscious thought behind them ending up in your shopping basket? Here are some typical ones:

- 'It's a bargain, so I'm saving money!' (By spending more?)

- 'I deserve it!' (What? Giving away your money?)

- 'They'll love me if I get them this!' (Please love me!)

- 'It's only one extra item!' (Who are you kidding?)

- 'No one will know.' (Self-deception)

- 'If I don't buy it now, it might not be available next week.' (Scarcity)

- 'I want it *now*!' (Witness the child in you!)

When I did this exercise, I discovered that I regularly bought more than I had planned to at the supermarket – I often succumbed to the 'three for the price of one' offers in the fruit and vegetable department. So, I switched my weekly shopping to the local greengrocers and now I spend a fraction of what I used to, I receive good-quality, locally grown produce, and there is less waste.

Decide on Your Income

Another example of giving away your money (read energy) unconsciously is in the way you do business, particularly if your business is your own. If you go to meet a prospective client, decide in advance on your perfect outcome (or *income* to be more accurate!), and how far you will choose to discount. Then, if you end up giving away too much – by doing a free talk, for example, rather than requesting your usual fee – it will have been driven by an unconscious choice.

Any deviance from your planned choice of outcome needs to be reviewed, and you need to ask yourself: 'Why did I make this unconscious choice; what was driving it?' There have been occasions when I have felt happy to accept less pay without an obvious equal exchange of value, and I've found that this has normally been driven by a desire to be liked. Being liked by others became more important to me than liking myself enough to be paid!

Of course, that's not how I would have expressed it at the time. I would have justified less money by saying that my mission was to help others, or to make a difference, or that 'what goes around comes around' – implying that I'd be looked after somehow, but effectively giving up on looking after myself in that moment!

■ Case Study: Align Yourself to Your True Worth

One of the wake-up calls for me came when I agreed to do a talk in Brighton for a small percentage of the door takings, plus takings from any book sales made on the night. A week before the event, I called the organizers to check how ticket sales were going and I was dismayed to discover that only nine tickets had been sold. It didn't take long for me to work out that what I was going to be paid wouldn't even cover my train fare to get there!

Now, I am driven by a passion to get my message out there so more people can see what's possible for them, but to do so while impoverishing myself lacked integrity. However, I had committed to the event and I had no intention of letting people down, so I explained that the situation didn't work for me, and requested expenses and a higher percentage of the door takings. The organizers agreed to my request for a higher percentage, even though it was more than they usually pay their speakers, and I was then energetically aligned and committed to it being a fantastic, transformational evening. By the time I arrived, the numbers had increased to 30, and it was indeed an amazing evening, for which I received my full value.

So, even if you have the most powerful message on the planet to deliver, if you can't support yourself financially, you will have less power to make a difference. If you have a powerful purpose or a passion, you also have a responsibility to look after yourself and your needs.

Being financially secure is not the opposite of helping others – it enables you to help others. Being financially free enables you to be of service, without any resentment or worry.

If you have your own business, get clear on your price *before* entering into any negotiation, promotional talk or business opportunity. Watch out for any unconscious pulls that cause you to lower your price while in conversation. If you see that you have a pattern of being nice, and accommodating your clients' needs on price, decide in advance that you will not be able to change the price, under any circumstances, during that meeting. You could set things up so that authorization or consultation with your colleagues is needed before any price change can be agreed. This will buy you a breathing space and help you to break your pattern.

Money Magnet Mindset Tool: Creating an Unplanned Expenditure Chart

Create a chart in your journal, or on a separate piece of paper. Split it into six columns with the following headings: Date; Amount spent; Recipient of your money (e.g. a shop or a professional); Value received in exchange (e.g. item bought or service received); Justification (for expenditure); Notes.

Now think of the last time that you spent money unconsciously. What was the reason for the spend? Write it down in the chart. Recall other occasions, and record them in the chart too. It may be particularly useful to record the *emotions* that you experienced at the time you spent the money, or what emotions you may have been looking to *avoid* by spending it.

You can also use the chart to record those instances where you have spent outside your planned expenditure for that day. This includes where you have not charged

the full price for your services. For example, if you
have stipulated from the outset that you plan to offer a
discount to a customer and you offer the discount that
you specified, then you would not add this to the chart. If,
however, you gave away more than you'd planned, enter it
on the chart.

The purpose of this exercise is to uncover your
unconscious patterns of spending, and what is driving
them. This will give you real power. You will start to
see what patterns are running your life, and, most
importantly, you will then be in a position to consciously
change them. Here is a sample chart:

Date	Amount	Recipient	Value Received	Justification	Notes
2/1	£5.99	H&M	Bikini	It was cheap!	Didn't need it
12/1	£125 (50% off fee)	Client	Appreciation	'Better one client at 50% than none.'	
18/1	£240	Jewellers	Necklace	'I deserve it!'	Time of the month
19/1	£35	Florist	A friend's gratitude	'I'm a loving person'	Lack of planning

No one else needs to see your Unplanned Expenditure Chart!
It's for you to see where you might be giving away more than

you receive, and are therefore financially out of balance. Remember, we are talking about unconscious patterns here, rather than saying there is anything wrong with giving in itself. Giving to charity, for example, should be a conscious decision and the exchange of value is clear. There are times when you will give on the spur of the moment, maybe because you feel compassion for someone. You get to help someone else and you end up feeling better about yourself as a person.

Become a Saver!

I have already recommended that, in terms of saving, you set up some direct debits to ensure you are saving regularly each month. However, to become more conscious of your beliefs around money, I suggest that you get yourself a piggy bank. Make a choice about how much money you wish to put into your piggy bank each day, and notice any resistance that you feel in fulfilling this small contract with yourself.

Will you go out of your way to find the right amount of change, or will you skip a day because you only have a banknote to hand? What justification will you give yourself for not saving each day with your piggy bank? What does it mean to you to save? For example, it might take you back to your childhood and having to do as you were told, and not wanting to! Just notice what comes up and keep choosing to put the money aside as a way of valuing yourself each day.

Once you have done the exercise to become aware of how you are unconsciously choosing to give away your money, I suggest that you turn your attention to how you can become more conscious of choosing to give *yourself* money.

Money Magnet Mindset Tool: Creating More Money for Yourself

Each day, jot down in your journal or notebook how much money you are going to create for yourself. This could be as a result of making some economies so you can keep some money for yourself, or finding a way to bring money in through effective negotiation, or selling more value.

Make sure you give yourself a good pat on the back for what you have achieved, and that you reinforce this positive behaviour with the affirmation: 'I now choose to have more money!'

■ Case Study: Become a Money Magnet Whenever You Wish!

Melanie called me up in a distressed state because her card had been rejected at the supermarket and she couldn't buy any food. Could I help her get some money that day?

I shared with Melanie what I have shared with a number of people who needed to manifest money very quickly. It's a technique that you can use time and time again, whenever you wish to become a Money Magnet. The funny thing is that most people just don't bother to use it all the time; they seem to save it up for emergencies. Anyway, let me run through with you the first step I used to help Melanie, and how you can use it to help yourself to more money whenever you wish.

Melanie told me that not only was she unable to buy any food, but her best friend was celebrating her 40th birthday with a weekend for friends in Malta and she couldn't afford to go. I asked her how much money she needed. *'Well, I need £400 for the weekend, so £500 would be good,'* she replied. So, she needed a minimum of £20 to buy food, and she wanted £500 to be able to buy food *and* join her friends on the holiday.

Then I asked her: *'What would be the sum of money that it would be totally fantastic to receive right now?'* to which she replied: *'If I could find £750, that would be absolutely brilliant.'* *'Okay,'* I said, *'let's go for the £750!'* I will share with you what we did next in Part 2, but the main thing is that you understand how important it is to be clear about what you want, and to choose an amount that inspires and uplifts you. Melanie received her £750 by the end of the day.

MONEY MAGNET MINDSET HABITS:
MONEY CHOICES

- Make daily choices that are aligned with you having more money.

- Become a savvy shopper.

- Use a piggy bank or two for your spare change.

- Keep a budget for your expenses and decide in advance how much to spend.

- Use shopping lists to become more conscious of your spending.

- Decide how much money you want in advance of a negotiation.

- Say 'no' more often to unnecessary expenditure.

- Create alternative, cheaper evenings out with friends.

- Look at planning your expenses to benefit from better deals.

- Make daily actions that are aligned with you having more money.

- Use the affirmation 'I now choose to have more money.'

PART 2

TAKING ACTION!

A man approached J.P. Morgan, held up an envelope and said, 'Sir, in my hand I hold a guaranteed formula for success, which I will gladly sell you for $25,000.' J.P. Morgan opened the envelope, and extracted a single sheet of paper. He gave it a mere glance, and then paid the man the agreed fee.

The paper read:
1. Every morning, write a list of the things that need to be done that day.
2. Do them.

Unknown

Chapter 5

Plan to Have More Money

'Reduce your plan to writing. The moment you complete this, you will have definitely given concrete form to the intangible desire.'
– **Napoleon Hill**

So, now you are clear about how much money you want, and the date when you will have it in your bank account. You are even clear on *why* you want the money. The only question left in your mind is: 'Yes, but how?!'

The first part of any new journey is the choice of destination, followed by the planning of the route. Of course, some people will always take the 'Thelma and Louise' route, but look what happened to them! Seriously, if you want to get anywhere in life, whether it's from Liverpool to New York or from the entrance of the shopping mall to your favourite store, you need to know where you're going and have a plan that will get you there.

When Melanie called me, she just wanted a way to have more money quickly. She hadn't worked out how much money. She was in a panic and was simply in the space of desperately wanting more money. In that state of mind, it would have been virtually impossible for her to attract any money at all!

This is the dilemma of the person who desperately needs more money. They are coming from an emotional place rather than an inspired one. All their focus is on the negative emotion of feeling needy, rather than on the positive emotion of feeling inspired and creative.

Melanie realized that she needed help to shift her mindset. When you can't see a way out of your current situation, it's because you are so wrapped up in it that you find it impossible to step back for long enough to find a solution. The thinking that got you into the situation is not going to get you out of it, either. In those circumstances, it is of course imperative that you ask someone else for help.

Write Down Your Goals

Whether you need someone like a coach to get you clear on your goals, or whether you already have an idea of what you want, the important thing is to *write it down*. This is imperative. Once we'd established that Melanie's goal was to find £750 by the end of the day, we were able to answer the 'how?' question by putting together a written plan for the day to achieve the goal.

Living life without goals is like sitting on a train until you decide to get off. You could end up anywhere and in the meantime, you're likely to keep going round in circles!

■ Case Study: The Power of Goal Setting

Tererai Trent was born in a small hut in a village in Zimbabwe, southern Africa. She doesn't know when she was born, as there is no documentation, but she thinks it may have been 1965. Tererai was not allowed to go to school but she studied from her brother's books and was soon doing his homework. When the teacher found out, she managed to persuade Tererai's parents to allow her to attend school for a few terms, but then she was married off at the tender age of 11. Tererai's husband banned her from going to school, and beat her if he caught her reading just a scrap of newspaper.

Then Jo Luck (what a perfect name!) arrived in the village. Jo was president of the charity Heifer International, and she started to talk to the village women about achieving their goals. The women were puzzled when she asked them what their hopes were, because they didn't have any hopes. As Jo pushed them to think about their dreams, Tererai timidly expressed a desire to be educated. Jo seized the moment to tell her that she could do anything if she wrote down her goals and methodically pursued them.

So Tererai wrote down her goals. They included going to America, and achieving a college degree, a

Master's degree and a PhD – all ridiculously absurd dreams for a married cattle-herder with five children and less than a year's formal education. You can read the full story of Tererai in the book *Half the Sky: How to Change the World* by Nicholas D. Kristoff and Sheryl Wudunn, but you might have already guessed the incredible outcome of her story.

Against all odds, Tererai went on to travel to the US, where she earned her degree. She came back to her village and dug up the list of goals that she had buried years earlier in a safe place and ticked off the goals she had achieved. When she achieved her Master's degree she returned again to tick it off her list. Tererai is now studying for her PhD and lives in the US with her children. Her dissertation will be about AIDS programmes for the poor in Africa. She will become a productive economic asset for Africa, and all because she was once introduced to the idea of writing down her hopes as goals that could be ticked off as she achieved them.

Now, if that story doesn't inspire you to sit down right away and write out your goals – no matter how crazy they may seem – then I don't think you will ever write out your goals! Consider the wealth in your life right now, and wake up to the resources you have to achieve your dreams. You can achieve anything you like in your life, and as much money as you truly desire, once you get clear on your goals and write them down.

Goals can be set for any period of time. They can be set for the outcome of a short sales meeting, or for the next five or even ten years of your life. A lot of people review their goals at the start of each year, which is traditionally a time for new resolutions and a surge of resolve. I recommend that you include goals for the forthcoming year, and also for the next 3–5 years at least. You will find that a three-year goal, once written down, can be achieved in say, 18 months, but if it's not captured, then it is unlikely to be achieved at all. Once you anchor a goal by writing it down, your mind can get into action to find ways to achieve it.

Sara heard me talking about how Elaine had set the intention of attracting £1million in three months. *'I want to manifest £20,000 in three months for schools in India,'* she told me. *'Am I thinking too small?'* Well, the fact that she had asked this question meant that yes, she *was* thinking too small. I asked her, *'What comes to mind when you shift your goal to achieving £1million in three months?'*

Sara looked at me, and within seconds she replied: *'Well, my brother-in-law is director of one of the world's biggest search engine companies in the US...'* Can you see that her mind, once given the larger goal of £1million, had simply found the resources that she needed to access to make it happen?

Don't allow your goals to be compromised by what you think is possible. Allow yourself to grow into the possibility of your goal. Who would you need to become to be a millionaire, for example? You as a millionaire would be quite different from the you that you are now.

See Yourself Achieving Your Goals

Take a moment out of reading this book to sit quietly for a few moments and visualize yourself achieving your goals.

What does it feel like to have won that gold medal, or to have £1million in the bank, or to run that global business? What type of person have you become? What advice do you have for the current you, who is looking to follow the steps of a plan to get there?

Money Magnet Mindset Tool: Cheat Time and Have the Money Now!

Allocate time each day to visualizing yourself having achieved your financial target – let's say it is £1million.

What is the first thing you will do once you hear that you have secured the £1million?

How do you hear the news?

Who is the first person you will tell? Can you see yourself making the phone call, and feel the emotion contained in your words as you share your news with that person?

Or are you picturing yourself visiting someone so you will be able to see their face when you tell them that you've done it? That you got there against all the odds!?

You defied the sceptics. You trusted yourself to achieve what you set out to achieve.

Enjoy the feelings of success – now!

What the mind can conceive the mind can achieve. In fact, studies have shown that there is little difference between an athlete *imagining* doing their training and actually *doing* the training. Britain's Dame Kelly Holmes, double gold Olympic medal winner, said: *'I know that my body is strong enough. It is all just down to the mind now.'* You can train your mind every day to be successful.

Goals that inspire you will transform you.

A wise person once told me that you should never accept a new job that you already know you can do easily. Always go for something that will stretch you, and that will expand your value and your view of yourself.

Money Magnet Mindset Tool: Living Your Vision of Success

Take a moment to summarize your aspirational goals for the coming year. And then add your specific financial goals. Unlike Terarai, you don't need to hide your goals under a rock; in fact, I recommend that you reproduce your list of goals on a small card that you can carry with you at all times.

By .... 20......... I will be so happy to have achieved the following (insert key goals):

....

....

....

....

....

....

My friend Chantal has written her goals on small note cards, which she keeps in a small wallet that she carries with her. Her goals include personal financial goals as well as her visions of travelling into space and having everyone in the world reduce their consumption of meat.

If you own a business, you should have a business plan, and the first step of any business plan is to define the Mission and Vision of the business. In other words, what the business does and where is it going. Write it down now and start sharing it with your employees, your clients, and anyone who has contact with your business. Be proud of your vision for the business!

The Mission of my business is to: (For example: 'Provide resources that will inspire and motivate people to achieve their full potential value.')

....

....

The Vision of my business is to: (For example: 'Have 100 Money Magnet coaches worldwide who will make a significant impact on eradicating global poverty.')

....

....

Creating a Plan of Action

Okay, so now that you have written out your aspirational and financial goals, the next step is to have a plan to achieve them. Please note that you should *always* have the aspirational goal written down *before* you even think about a plan for achieving it. With the financial goal it is important that you are not yet 100% clear on how you are going to achieve it. To be honest, part of the fun of this exercise is being curious about how you can find a way you've never thought of before to achieve the money!

Some people write down how much money they want, and yet they never go on to achieve it. In the worst cases, not achieving their stated goal sends them into a spiral of despair, as they lose confidence in themselves and lose faith in a system that seems to work for everyone else.

The most common reasons given for not achieving an aspirational goal include:

- 'I don't have enough time.'

- 'I don't have enough money.'

- 'I can't do it all.'

- 'I'm not 100% sure about the idea.'

- I'm not sure I'm doing the right thing.'

- I'm not 100% sure I can do it.'

- 'There are better people out there doing the same thing.'

- 'I've lost faith.'

- 'It'll never earn me enough money.'

- 'I don't know how to take it to the next level.'

- 'I'm scared of taking the next step.'

- 'It is too much hard work/responsibility.'

- 'I've decided that it isn't about the money after all (read any of the above!)

Are any of the above the reason why you're not yet a millionaire, or why you've not yet written your book, or started your business, or bought an investment property?

Now, if I was to tell you that having a written plan would solve not one but all of the above issues, would you be interested? Yes, of course you would! For those of you who haven't just thrown the book aside and rushed to grab a pen and paper to get started on your plan straight away, allow me to elaborate.

'I don't have enough time'

We all have the same amount of time as the next person. We all start with the same amount of resource. It is the way in which we use this precious resource that will determine the level of our wealth. If you spend your time creating something, like a book or a product, it is time well spent if that book or product can then be duplicated and sold time and time again to help as many people as possible.

If your time is spent helping or loving others in a way that makes your heart sing, it is time well spent. If your time is spent doing something that fulfils you and helps you to grow as a person, it is time well invested in you.

Time is like money. If you waste it on things that don't serve you, there will be an impact. If you use it wisely, and delegate where possible, you'll maximize your value from time, and you will be rich. Start to become responsible for each hour of your day. Just like you did in an earlier exercise in becoming conscious of how you eat or spend your money unconsciously, a plan is the tool to make you more conscious of the time available to you, and where you are currently wasting your time.

Money Magnet Mindset Tool: Valuing Your Time and Using it Wisely

Step 1: Set your alarm clock for one-hour intervals during the day, and note down how you spent your time in each hour. If you can, do this for five typical days, in order to get a real idea of how you are currently spending your time.

Step 2: Create a daily timesheet and split it into separate portions of time – e.g. 60- to 90-minute slots – and schedule your activities according to your goals and priorities. For example, if you want to attract more money, make sure you schedule in time to review your accounts, make sales calls or review the effectiveness of your website.

Step 3: Stick to your plan! Plan your time and make sure that you time yourself doing the plan, stopping when you have finished the allocated time slot. This is an excellent tool to train your mind into achieving results within a limited time slot. It allows you much more time to have fun and enjoy life (instead of feeling guilty when you're not working because you don't know when everything is going to get done).

Managing your time by following a simple plan means that you can book in holidays and time off when it suits you best, *and* still know that everything is getting done and that you are making progress on your goals each day.

'I don't have enough money'

If you don't have enough money to do something – like Melanie with her friend's birthday holiday – you need to ask yourself: 'How can I have more money?' And then make a plan to have more money!

The ideas that Melanie came up with for earning more money included creating websites, dog walking, delivering workshops and doing bar work. She then focused on creating websites and wrote down a plan of action. This included a long list of people she would call to find some website work, and scheduled times when she planned to make those calls. She followed the plan, made the calls, and found the work that would pay her the money!

Maybe you need money to invest in your product or money-earning idea and you don't know where to find it. Start pretending that you *do* know, and just start writing your plan to find the money. You may be surprised by the ideas and resources you come up with once you put your mind to it. Make sure that you write the plan in terms of a series of actions to be completed by a certain date, and make sure that you complete the actions!

'I can't do it all'

When we have big dreams and goals, it can seem a little overwhelming. We start to wonder how we can possibly fit it all in. Maybe you want to start your own business on top of a full-time job and it just feels like you can't possibly do it all. Again, by writing a plan you can organize how you spend your time, and what other resources or people you can employ to make the best use of your time.

Maybe you don't actually have to do it all. What are the areas that you can delegate to others? Allocate all the tasks of the plan to the relevant people. Once you have a full plan in place with a team to support you, and everyone knows their part in the overall plan, all each person needs to do is to follow their part of the plan and the whole is accomplished effortlessly within the set timescales.

'I'm scared of taking the next step'

Sit down and write a plan of the next actions you would take if you *knew* what actions to take. Make the steps teeny-weeny little ones if need be, and then just take one step at a time. Get a coach to help you if you are really stuck.

'I'm not sure I'm doing the right thing'

If you wait until you are 100% certain in life, it could take you a very long time to get anything done! Once you have a plan, all you need to do is follow it. You won't need to think about it anymore. If it is the wrong plan, something will come up to stop you in your tracks and you will know instinctively when to change tack. But if you never get started, you'll never know.

Money Magnet Mindset Tool: Deciding on a Course of Action

If you're not sure what to do next, decide by flipping a coin.

As soon as the coin is in the air, you will know exactly what you really want to do!

'I've decided that it isn't about the money after all'

Whatever your aspirational goal, having a financial goal as well allows you to accurately track your progress. So, make sure that you write down your financial goal at the top of your plan of action. You're right, it's not necessarily about the money, but money is probably the most effective measure of success. It doesn't lie and it grounds your dreams in reality.

Sometimes people tell me that they run a successful business, but on questioning them I find that the business is not actually making any money. A successful business is defined by how many people want to pay a certain amount of money for a product or services. The amount of money people are prepared to pay has to be significantly more than the amount of money it costs the business to make those products and services.

If everybody wants your services but they are not prepared to pay a decent price in exchange for them, then it is unlikely that your business is successful. You may be busy, but you are not valuing what you do, and neither are your customers. This type of business is unsustainable.

How do you find out how good you are at your job? By testing to see how much people are prepared to pay you to do the job. There is always money available for somebody who brings additional value.

By including a monetary measure of your success within your plan, there will be no doubt whether you achieve the target or not. You'll know the exact moment for celebration! Money provides clarity, and it provides focus. Once you have the financial targets in place, you are free to concentrate on everything that you do well, irrespective of the money conversation.

Lots of people tell me that they want to focus on doing the business rather than managing the money! That would be like choosing to walk wishfully in a direction rather than taking a car and a map to get you to your destination. Having a plan in place allows you to focus on the business within a structure that will deliver the results you want. As long as you have targets and measures in place that are regularly reviewed, you can relax and enjoy what you do, knowing that each step you take will get you to your desired destination.

A plan frees you up to enjoy each moment of what you do, while knowing that you are on track to achieve all your goals.

One of the ways that my sales team was always able to achieve over £1million sales revenue a month was by using a wall chart in the office to track our daily sales performance against the monthly target. At any given point, everyone could see what was still to be done to achieve the target. It kept the whole team focused on achieving the goal. When you are really focused, you can reach *any* goal that you set yourself!

Money Magnet Mindset Tool: Tracking Your Success

What is your monthly money target?

Create a Performance Chart to keep a daily track of your results against your monthly money target. Give it a heading like 'Monthly Money-IN Target' and add columns for Date; Name of Item; Amount of Money In; Cumulative Amount of Money.

MONEY MAGNET MINDSET HABITS: PLAN TO HAVE MORE MONEY

- At any time, have your daily, monthly, annual and longer-term financial goals written down.

- Allocate specific time slots for each day, ideally defined the previous evening.

- Don't forget to plan in time for contingencies, holidays, pleasure and relaxation.

- Plan in times to train your mind for success by visualizing your desired outcomes.

- Find ways to delegate tasks in a day so you can maximize the value of your time.

- Say 'no' to activities that distract you from your main focus.

- Schedule a regular time each month to review your performance and plans.

- Reward yourself whenever you meet any of your financial targets.

- Break down your plan into smaller chunks.

- Be prepared to change a plan if it requires some flexibility.

- Don't delay taking any action because the plan isn't complete.

Chapter 6

Inspir-action!

'We can't solve problems by using the same kind of thinking we used when we created them.'
– **Albert Einstein**

A few years back there was a film, and then a book, called *The Secret*. They were a global success and their premise was that you can have anything you wish for in life. All you need to do is to be clear on what you want, align yourself to your desires, and hey presto, the universe will deliver. The message was not incorrect, but it was confusing. People rushed out to create vision boards and to practise affirmations of wealth, but then they were disappointed when nothing happened.

The film showed a man moving into a magnificent new home with his family and then spotting that he had stuck a picture of this exact home on his vision board some years earlier. What it *didn't* show were all the actions that he'd taken over the years in order to get the house. It didn't show the challenges he'd faced and overcome to become the type of man who would own a house like that, and it didn't show the sacrifices that he had made along the way. It showed the glittering prize without disclosing the triumphant fight. It's like much of the advertising that surrounds us, which says, 'You can have this house and not pay a deposit', or 'You can lose weight by buying this exercise machine.' Both contain an essential missing ingredient.

In Feng Shui, we look at how the energy of our environment affects us, whether it's the astrology of our birth or the internal decoration of our home or office. However, it is the energy of man, connecting heaven and Earth, that is the catalyst for miracles.

It is when you connect inspiration with action that you bring to life new possibilities.

This is not to say that I do not believe in the miracle of prayer. I witness miracles and magical coincidences too often to deny that miracles do happen. However, in my experience, if you are serious about maintaining a Money Magnet Mindset you will become a person of action.

Big Energy = Big Money!

Look at any successful entrepreneur who is relaxed and happy and you will see someone who has high energy and a passion for life. They cram each day with joy and creativity and action. They squeeze the juice out of life and drink it daily. It's as though they have a natural fountain of happiness that springs from their heart and affects everybody around them.

Contrast that with the hard-working executive who has no energy left at the end of the day, is always striving to be good enough, and who looks to alcohol or TV or some other diversion to pick himself up. He is being busy and active, but he is not inspired by what he does. Inside, he suspects that there must be a better way, but he is too scared to get off the treadmill for long enough to check it out. He is not lit up. He is using up all his energy running around in circles rather than pausing just long enough to hear the voice of inspiration.

He may earn lots of money but without expert advice, he is just as likely to spend away everything he earns. He cannot afford to listen to the expert advice, as that would mean admitting that he doesn't know everything. It would mean trusting someone else, and while he can't trust himself to make the right choices in life, it will be impossible for him to trust another.

The harder he works, the more he feels the need to comfort himself with expensive toys and holidays abroad. He is not happy and the money he earns will never make him happy. It is only by taking action aligned with your heart's desires that you will be happy. And it is only when you are happy and value yourself that you will find the easy way to earn, keep and grow the money you earn.

Redundancy is often a welcome opportunity to take a pause and evaluate where you are in life. If you can embrace the initial feelings that come with losing a secure job, and your fear of the big blank canvas that is now in front of you, and see it instead as a God-given opportunity that you have created to paint a new picture for your life, then you will be blessed.

Rosemary was made redundant no fewer than ten times before she finally got the message. With each redundancy she would get straight out there and find almost the exact same job without pausing long enough to question if this was really the type of job she actually wanted to do. She was taking action as many of us have been taught to do. What she needed to do was to take *inspired* action, rather than keep doing what she'd always done. Most of us keep treading the treadmill of life, doing the same thing over and over again.

If you want to increase the amount of money you have, you are going to have to do something different to what you have been doing to date. Rosemary had been a corporate sales executive for as long as she could remember. Finally, something clicked after her tenth redundancy, and she paused just long enough to listen to her heart and to find out what she really wanted to do and what really inspired her. She then took some inspired action, instead of following the same pattern of action that she'd always taken.

> *Your level of wealth is not determined by how much you earn. It is determined by how much you have left at the end of each month to invest in yourself.*

Rosemary is now working to help the unemployed rediscover their self-esteem and get back on track. She can use her personal experience of redundancy to empathize with her clients and she feels one hundred times more fulfilled in this role. Rosemary used to waste her money on impressing others and her time on getting other people to love her. Now that she is honouring and loving herself, she values her time and money much more and as a result is now much richer, even though, technically, she earns less than she used to as a commercial salesperson.

The Missing Ingredient in **The Secret**

Taking inspired action is the missing ingredient from *The Secret*. It is the secret to enjoying a rich and fulfilled life. If your intention is to be wealthy, it is the key to you manifesting wealth.

Remember Melanie, who couldn't think what to do while she was in a state of panic and had a desperate need for money? If you are worried about debt, or about how you are going to pay your next month's rent, for example, your worry will stifle the young buds of inspiration. Worry grows like a weed. The more you water it, the more it will strangle the buds of your natural creativity. Love conquers fear.

To be inspired, you have to come from a place of total love.

Choose to love your debt, and the challenges you face each month.

Choose to love yourself and your life as it is right now.

Choose to trust your inner knowing, and give yourself the space to hear the quiet, still voice of inspiration. The more you act on your intuition, the more you will start to trust it, and your life will become one of joy, creativity and action.

Taking Action on a Great Idea

It is not enough just to have a great idea – we all have great ideas. How many times have you had one only to then see someone else deliver it? Next time you have a great idea, ask yourself whether it is aligned in some way with your priorities and values and whether you feel inspired and excited when you think about it?

Money Magnet Mindset Tool: Turning Ideas into Action

What is your great idea? Write it down now.

....

What specific actions do you need to take to make it happen?

....

....

....

Are you willing to commit yourself 100% to making it real?

....

If the answer to the third question is 'no', ask yourself what would need to happen for the answer to become 'yes'.

It may be that it's an idea to sell to someone else, or it's an idea that is the precursor to a much bigger one. It may

be that you're scared to take the necessary actions or that you think you can't do it?

Ask yourself why you think you had this idea.

The bottom line is that if you have an inspired thought that lights you up, the odds are you've received the thought because you are the person to fulfil on it and to make it real in the world. Choose to love the idea, and to trust that you are the best person to make it happen, one way or another.

■ *Case Study: Businesses Grow Out of Inspired Ideas*

Louie Adshead is a successful property investor who also runs her own dog training business called Trainthatdog. One day, when looking at an old single bed that had belonged to her father and was soon to be put on the bonfire, she came up with the idea of turning it into a dog bed. This idea developed into the dog bed becoming a smart piece of furniture for the home, complete with elegant Queen Anne legs. Louie trusted herself to know that there was likely to be a market for such an item, and so she and her partner designed the first prototype based on the style of the old single bed. That one simple idea translated into a money-making business called The Dog Bed Company. The company now supplies a range of handmade wooden dog beds to lots of very lucky dogs up and down the UK.

Now, in order to make that idea a reality, Louie had to create more time in her already busy life. She had to find people who could make the beds in quantity, and partners who were willing to sell them for her. She had to learn new ways of market promotion, such as social media, and she had to be prepared to ask for help in the areas where she had no knowledge. The additional money she makes from this business is a direct reflection of the value she offered in the product, but it is also a reflection of how she had to expand as a person to make it happen.

Bruce lives in the English countryside, where he is the owner of two businesses – a marquee company and a building firm. From working with a lot of farmers, he knew the problems they encountered from inadequate security on their land. It isn't easy to securely lock a typical farmer's gate. Then one day Bruce came up with an idea for a fail-safe fence lock that would solve the problem for the farmers. Having sketched out the design, he found someone to make up a prototype and had 50 made up to find out if they would sell. The lock is called the Zedlock, and it has proved incredibly popular already among the farmers of Sussex!

Now what would have happened if Louie and Bruce had not acted on their ideas? What would have happened if neither the dog bed nor the lock had been successful? Louie and Bruce might have felt they'd wasted some time and money, but time is rarely wasted on developing original ideas. There is always learning to be had from trying out new things, and being prepared to investigate what might be possible.

That's how Thomas Edison came up with the lightbulb, and how James Dyson invented the Dyson vacuum cleaner. The only waste for them would have been if they had come up with the ideas and not done anything about them, maybe thinking that they hadn't got enough time to start a new business on top of what they were already doing.

If you can dream it, you can achieve it.

Give Yourself Permission to Dream of What Might Be Possible

At school we are told off for daydreaming and yet dreaming of new possibilities will give you access to new ideas and inspiration. Why do you think Richard Branson makes a point of taking months out of his work schedule to relax with his family?

Richard Branson dreams of taking us into space. He is inspired by how space travel will change our perception of the world we live in, and he took immediate action on his dream. He registered the company 'Virgin Galactic' and set out to find the right person and the money to make it happen.

When you are committed to a course of action, the miracles show up. When you are committed to an idea, the money will show up. Ask any serious property investor. They don't wait for the money. They buy the property and then find the money. Richard found someone to oversee the technology involved and he then succeeded in winning an initial £12million grant to get started. Galactic travel is now becoming a real possibility! What would you do if you knew you could make it possible?

Money Magnet Mindset Tool: Stop Waiting for the Money!

What have you always said you would do if you had enough money to do it?

....

....

Now write down the date that you are committed to doing it by:

....

What if you don't know what to do? Or even worse, you have so many ideas that you don't know which one to act on first? Most people always do what they've always done. Finding out what you really want to do and then acting on it can be very challenging, especially if you have always done what you think others want you to do.

Go With What Makes You Happy

Sometimes we get so caught up with the pressures of life and what we think we need to do just to keep our ship afloat that we lose track of what we really want to do and what makes us happy. When I suspect that I may have veered off track and I am no longer aligned with my best self, I do the following exercise. It clears out the metaphorical weeds and plants the seed of your full promise.

Write a list of everything you've ever been inspired to be, do, or have. Try to come up with more than 100 ideas or things.

Look at life as you did when you were a child, when anything and everything was possible. Did you dream of being a TV star or an astronaut? If Richard Branson can dream of space travel, what is your biggest, most outlandish dream?

My dream is of a world in which everyone is happy and free to be themselves. Your dreams are what get you out of bed and into action each morning. Every time I make a difference to an individual and leave them feeling more enriched, I am inspired to do more and to look at how I can reach more people. It is a wonderful way to live your life. Work no longer feels like hard work. Life takes on a new richness and you become richer every day.

Money Magnet Mindset Tool: Finding Your Top Heart's Desire

Once you have your list of over 100 ideas, go through it two items at a time, choosing the item that inspires you most.

Keep choosing until you have filtered the list down to your top heart's desire.

Don't worry about whether it's possible or not.

Don't listen to the voice in your head that says you have to do item 1 before you can complete item 2.

(A mother doing this exercise with me faltered because she had to choose between helping her children to eat better or losing weight herself. Her head said that the children should come first, but her heart wanted her to lose the weight herself first. Can you see how the heart's choice would benefit everyone?)

One way to stop you choosing with your head rather than your heart is to ask a friend to give you the options two at a time and to rush you into answering. Their job is to make sure that you don't have time to think and to challenge you when they suspect that your head has got involved. Alternatively, you can download the app Heart's Desire, which will do this work for you once you have entered in your heart's desires.

When I first did this exercise, my list was full of grand ideas to change the world. I was then somewhat dismayed to find that my top heart's desire was to lose weight. 'How superficial!' I thought. But when we trust ourselves to listen to that inner voice of wisdom, we know exactly what to do and we can get into action immediately.

I then honoured my number one heart's desire to lose weight. I started to be responsible about what I ate. Gradually, my eating habits changed, and I started to take more exercise. Like lots of people, I knew what to do to lose weight. I just hadn't been committed until that point. I hadn't taken the necessary action!

As the weight dropped off and I was eating more healthily, my confidence and self- esteem grew and I was then ready for the next item on the list!

If your top heart's desire is to be wealthy, you will then take the necessary actions and attract the perfect resources and opportunities to make you rich. If, however, your first heart's desire is something other than wealth, honour it. In stating your wealth goal in advance, your heart or inner voice will then lead you magically and easily to the wealth you desire. All you need to do is to listen to your inner voice, take action and trust in the outcome.

Using this tool with clients over the years, I have watched as their wealth has increased, not just from working hard to have more money, but by listening to their inner voice and taking inspired action. Invariably, you will end up fulfilling most of your stated desires, but in choosing to take an inspired route where you trust yourself and your choices, it happens in a much easier way than you'd imagine and in a way that reinforces your personal value and self-esteem.

The Four Essential Steps

Here are four steps you can take on a daily basis to maintain a healthy Money Mindset:

1. State your monetary goal (one that excites you!)

2. Listen to your inner voice to find the 'how'.

3. Take inspired action.

4. Trust in the outcome.

State your monetary goal

If you don't get clear on your desired outcome first, you risk spending your day just being busy and creative but never making a difference to the amount of money that you have. I have come across lots of people who have followed their hearts and are doing what they love but who complain that they are now not earning as much money. There are lots of reasons for this, of course. For example, they may have a belief that you have to suffer at work in order to earn decent money. However, the simplest explanation is that they haven't specified how much money they want.

We covered goals and intentions in Part 1 so you should have your overall financial goal by now. What I encourage you to do now is to have a daily financial goal.

How much money are you going to attract today?

....

Choose a figure that inspires you. Not so unrealistic that you have a built-in reason why it's not going to work, but a figure that would stretch you a little. Remember, what you focus on expands! Focus on the amount of money you are going to attract today. Write it down in your journal and commit to achieving it, even if you have no idea how you are going to achieve it! To keep this light and creative, you may want to think of the exercise as more of a game to play than hard work.

Listen to your inner voice to find the 'how'

Now that you have declared your financial intention, you can let it go and get on with the day. To come from an inspired place during the day I encourage you to stay fully focused on whatever you are doing when you are doing it, and to schedule in times when your mind is allowed to wander.

For example, I love to break for lunch and spend half an hour in the kitchen preparing my food. During this time I allow the events of the morning to percolate and new ideas to take root in my mind. Similarly, I find that starting the day at the gym or taking a walk outside in the afternoon provides a new perspective on what I am up to. Stay alert for inspiration throughout the day.

New inspiration can pop up at the most extraordinary moments. It can happen mid-conversation with someone, or you can schedule in regular brainstorming sessions with colleagues and start training your brain to get creative at those specific times of day. The key thing is to capture the inspiration when it comes. I therefore recommend that you carry a special 'Ideas and Inspiration' notebook with you at all times. Note down every idea as it comes into your conscious mind.

It might be worth mentioning that the notebook should not then automatically become a 'to do' list. That would be exhausting and it could unconsciously stop you from writing down all your ideas.

The very act of writing down an idea anchors it in reality. At the end of each day or week you can then choose which ideas you are going to take action on, which you will schedule to take action on later, and which ideas you choose not to take any action on at all. This gives you permission to dream as broadly as you wish without feeling that you are then bound to follow through on everything.

Money Magnet Mindset Tool: Prioritizing Your 'To Do' Lists

You don't have to do it all right now! Prioritize your 'to dos' as follows:

Actions to be taken now.

Actions to be scheduled for a later date.

Actions that you will never take.

Take inspired action

Take action on the actions you have scheduled for the day. There is no better boost for your self-esteem and wealth than taking action and doing what you said you were going to do. You will feel your chest swell with pride and that energetic boost will attract more opportunities and wealth to you. You become someone who is worthy of receiving wealth and you then start to expect it.

The more action you take, particularly in areas where you are initially fearful or lacking in confidence, the more you will grow and expand your personal value.

Look at the three actions that will make the biggest difference to you feeling good at the end of the day and take those actions first. Brian Tracey refers to it in his famous book as needing to 'Eat That Frog!' The longer you look at the frog and think about how disgusting it would be to eat it, the longer it will be before you do eat it. In the meantime, the fear and dread will increase and the odds of you actually never doing the task will increase.

For many people, a tax return might be a typical 'frog' for them to eat each year. The more they talk about it, and moan about having to do it, the worse the task appears to be. And yet when they actually sit down and fill out the form, they discover how straightforward it is to complete. Best of all is the feeling of satisfaction, and even pride, when they know they have completed their tax return on time!

Always focus on the outcome of the task, and how great you will feel once you have done what you said you were going to do!

Money Magnet Mindset Tool: Eat that Frog!

Instead of thinking about the one dreaded action all day, and wasting your precious energy worrying about it, choose to do it first thing in the morning.

You will receive a boost in self-confidence and personal value that will carry you effortlessly, and even joyously, through the rest of the day's actions!

Now you perceive yourself to be someone of value, you will start to attract more value and appreciation from others.

Using a daily 'to do' list is an effective Money Magnet Mindset tool, but watch out that you are not just being busy. The feeling of satisfaction you get when you tick an item off is seductive and it's easy to fill your list with relatively easy actions that won't make the slightest difference to your wealth position but will give you a temporary buzz. Most people will go for the easy items first! Instead, I recommend that you devise your daily 'to do' lists so they are aligned with the personal goals that you set yourself in Part 1.

Here's an example:

Personal Goal	Today's Actions
Achieve £10,000 per month.	Call three prospective clients, redo CV.
Drop a dress size.	Join exercise class, shop at greengrocers.
Start a relationship.	Join a dating website; schedule a social activity.
Start a new business.	Schedule a meeting with a mentor.

Once you have attended to your main goals with whatever actions inspire you, then you can fill up your list with whatever you desire. It is only by taking lots of small actions each day that you make efficient progress towards achieving your goals. The trick here is to be *committed* to yourself and your dreams. The good news is that when you start doing this, the miracles start showing up and things get easier and easier!

For example, if you have set yourself a financial target of £5,000 by the end of the week, if you take an action each day towards this target, the chances are that you will then experience a lucky tax refund, or an unexpected gift that will achieve your target. The trick is to take regular inspired action.

Keep your focus on the end point, rather than on the perceived struggle to get there, and you will easily attract the money or the dream that you desire.

For Melanie to achieve her £750, she needed to take immediate action inside of her commitment to achieve the money by the end of the day. We had established at least three different ways she could attract the money, and she was inspired to write a list of people who she already knew might have an interest in employing her to do some website work.

Her action was to call each name on that list. To do so, she had to give up any fear she had about picking up the phone and calling these people. Above all else she had to give up her feeling of desperation. Nobody likes to buy from someone who is desperate to sell to them! So, Melanie stayed focused on what she could offer of value to each client, and with her financial goal in the back of her mind, she was able to ask for the business.

Melanie found some work and called me at lunchtime that very day to say that she had found her £750! By simply taking action on the names she'd been inspired to write down, the money had showed up! Remember, you already have access to the solution to any problem you are currently facing, especially those of a financial nature. You just need to listen to that inner voice of inspiration.

Trust in the outcome

While taking action is an essential ingredient in attaining more money, there also needs to be a balance with not taking action. In nature, we witness the balance of yin and yang all the time: night and day, sun and moon, male and female. If you are always pushing for results, there is no space to then receive the bounty of your efforts. A simple example of this is when you have someone who is full of compliments for you, so much so that there is no space to pay *them* a compliment.

If a salesperson is constantly pushy, and telling you why you should buy an item, there is no space for you to decide that you would in fact like to buy the item. If you desperately want a pay rise, you need to put forward your case and then allow some time for the decision to be reached. There may be a number of considerations to be taken into account, and if you push for an immediate decision you may lose out.

It is a fine balance between push and pull. This book is about being in the space of a Money Magnet, where money finds its way to you because of who you are, the thoughts you have, and the actions you take.

It's not about the old ways of greed and manipulation. It's not about bulldozing your way to success. It's about the feminine energy of intuition and flow combining with the masculine energy of focus and action. So make sure you plan in times of non-action where you are open to receiving.

MONEY MAGNET MINDSET HABITS: STAY INSPIRED AND HAPPY!

- Practise listening to and honouring your inner voice each day.

- Do things that feel right, even when they may not appear logical.

- Capture everything that you want by writing it down.

- Use the Heart's Desire exercise or app to know what to do first.

- Plan time out to do things that just make you happy.

- Choose to love everything about where you are right now.

- Keep an 'Ideas and Inspiration' journal.

- Take action on your ideas, even if the action is to add it to the list of 'no action to be taken' ideas.

- Do what you know in your heart you want to do.

- Every day, take actions aligned to your financial goals.

Chapter 7

Just Do It!

'Go as far as you can see; when you get there
you'll be able to see farther.'
– Thomas Carlyle

It doesn't actually matter how many books you read, how much you think and plan your fortune, or even who you know who can help you, if you never actually take any action towards your goal, you will never achieve the desired results.

Chloe attended a Money Magnet workshop where she cleared a deep-seated belief about her self-worth and her relationship with money. During the afternoon she created a new business idea and she was excited and thrilled at the possibility of earning a good income independent of her husband's. By the end of the day Chloe was full of ideas and actions she was going to take, and had attracted a number of people in the room who were happy to help her get the business off the ground.

Have you already guessed what happened next? When Chloe went back to her part of the country and away from the buzz of the group, it wasn't long before she'd talked herself out of doing anything. Her business idea evaporated into the ether, and will no doubt be found one day by somebody who *will* make it happen.

We're going to look a lot more at self-talk in Part 3, but in this case, all Chloe needed to do was take the first action on her plan – whether or not the little voice in her head said *'yes'* – and she would have launched herself into the path of destiny. To misquote Rod Stewart, 'the first step is the hardest', but once you take that first step, a new world of opportunity starts to open up. If you don't take the first step, you'll stay stuck in the same place all your life, just thinking and talking about doing stuff.

■ Case Study: Taking the First Step

Lizzie was a life coach who attended the same Money Magnet workshop as Chloe. She was in her fifties and married, with children who had long since left home. Her business had a few clients but it wasn't bringing in the income that she wanted. She needed something to reignite her passion and her joie de vivre.

Lizzie declared her intention to earn a specific amount of money, and she started to take actions to support her life coaching business. For example, she contacted a website designer with a view to finalizing her website. When we get into action, we shift our relationship to what's possible, and new ideas are able to infiltrate where there was previously no access.

Lizzie remembered a book she had read years earlier. It was Brian Tracey's *Eat that Frog!* After reading it again, she had the idea to run a workshop on the subject of the book – which is about overcoming procrastination – and she knew instinctively that there would be a huge market for it. We all have amazing ideas all of the time. Most people simply never take action to follow up their idea. Lizzie, by contrast, picked up the phone and called Brian Tracey's people in the US. Less than two weeks later, she had secured an exclusive UK license to run Eat that Frog workshops in the UK, and to train and recruit others to run them too!

Lizzie had found her niche market, and with the support of a well-known name and organization, she was now totally inspired by the difference she could make for others in this work. She also recognized the power of taking action, one step at a time. Along the way there were moments of fear – as she learnt how to deliver workshops and how to fill them with paying attendees – but as long as she kept taking action, the fear gradually subsided. The more actions she took in the direction of her vision, the more Lizzie embraced her new identity as a successful businesswoman.

One Step at a Time

If you have completed all the exercises so far, you will now know what actions you need to take. You will have your vision, your goals, and the plan of action that will get you there. All you need to do now is take one action at a time and congratulate yourself each day on the actions you have taken. If you feel fearful or stuck, I recommend that you invest in a personal coach who will give you the gentle push you need, and who will hold you accountable to even your wildest dreams!

If you haven't written down your goals and a plan to achieve them yet, you are resisting your life. You are pushing money away from you! If you didn't have the dream, it wouldn't matter – I would accept that you are happy with your life as it is, and that there is nothing missing. However, I suspect that you are reading this because you would like to change something about your life. You would like to have more money, right?

This book only works if you do what it recommends. The money only starts to come when you take a new action, whether it is clearing out the clutter in your home, writing a business plan or asking someone to invest in your business.

If you think about it, why would the universe give an amazing new money-making idea to someone who won't get off their butt to make their own idea work? So how do you let the universe know that you are ready for that £1million idea? You show that you are serious by taking immediate and consistent actions aligned with your current goals.

<u>Money Magnet Mindset Tool: Doing It Today!</u>

What action are you going to take today that you have been putting off until now?

....

Who are you going to call that you've been meaning to call for ages?

....

What can you envisage happening if all goes according to plan?

....

How will you feel having taken the action?

....

See it happening and *commit* to it now! Acknowledge the fantastic feeling of having done what you said you were going to do!

Look Beyond the Winning Line!

Keep your head up, metaphorically, and keep looking ahead beyond your desired outcome. Just as an Olympic athlete trains to win by visualizing themselves running past the winning line in record time, and ahead of all the other runners, you want to stay focused on your end outcome.

Do whatever you need to do to stay aligned with the positive outcome. Post up an image of the result where you can see it every day. Tell a trusted friend what you are *expecting* to happen. Take an action – for example, booking a holiday – that you would only take if you *knew* that you were going to achieve that outcome.

This is about you giving up anything and everything in your head that stands in the way of you achieving your end goal, so that you then start to expect to achieve it. The only way that you will discover what it feels like to be a person of higher value is to take the action step that a person of higher value would take... and just go for it!

Action Stoppers!

One of the most common reasons for not taking action is that we focus on what happens *before* taking the action (fear, apprehension, lack of information or knowledge about the outcome), or we focus on what will happen *while* taking the action (fear, looking stupid, upsetting someone, getting it wrong, not being able to retreat, failure).

Let's take a look at some most common action stoppers and some of the ways to overcome inaction:

Action Stopper	How To Overcome It
Focusing on failure	Keep visualizing and expecting a positive outcome
Fear of success	Focus on the achievement of one small step at a time
Negative self-talk	Change the way you talk to yourself (see Part 3)
Lack of trust	Do your research and due diligence; trust your intuition
Feeling emotionally challenged	Ground yourself with logic: touch something real, like a tree
Comparing yourself to others	Focus on your uniqueness and on your own specific goal
Feeling overwhelmed	Build a team around you and start delegating
Lack of experience	Employ a mentor who does have the experience

You started life with no experience of walking. However, inspired by the reward of extra food, or a hug from a delighted, loving parent, you were spurred on to take the necessary action. You literally took one step at a time. Even when you fell over repeatedly, and knocked your head, you carried on taking the action until you mastered walking. No one had taught you otherwise. You hadn't yet learnt how to give up on yourself, or how to be resigned about your life. At that young age you were full of hope and promise and possibility.

At the age when you wanted to ride a bicycle, you knew what to do. You needed to get on the bike and start trying to ride it. If you were lucky, you may have had someone to guide and coach you, and they may have invested in some stabilizers to give you more support during the early, most challenging stages. You knew that, sooner or later, you would be riding that bike, and that nothing was going to get in your way. All you needed to do was keep taking the necessary action.

Now, of course, you don't even need to think about the fact that you can ride a bike, or drive a car, or do whatever it is that you now do in life. You just do it. You have become the type of person who knows how to ride a bike, drive a car and do whatever it is you do for a living.

Now what if what you do for a living isn't earning you the amount of money you want? It may be time to choose to do something different. There is always an unlimited number of ways to make money. Whether you choose to become a doctor, an internet marketer, a trader of shares, a pop star or a property investor, you will always start off from the same place. Decide what it is that you want, and take the first step towards getting you there. Some journeys will take you longer than others, but if you just keep taking the action, one step at a time, you will learn along the way. Resist taking action and you will become a wishful thinker who is missing out on the real juice of your life.

'If you think you can't…you must!'
– Mark Dalton

I love that phrase. Write it out and put it somewhere where you'll see it clearly at those moments when you are terrified of taking the next step. The thing about fear is that it disappears the moment you face up to it. It is the ultimate coward. Don't ever tolerate the bullying voice of fear when it has no power. If your life is genuinely under threat, you will act instinctively. At all other times, fear can be summarized like this:

FEAR = False Evidence Appearing Real.

Take the action and you'll find out what I mean. Resist taking the action and you'll stay at the scary edge of the abyss all your life, wondering what could have happened but terrified of taking the next step. Living your life in a state of fear is to live a nightmare. All you need to do is to take the first step.

Take a Leap

One of my favourite films is *Papillon,* starring Steve McQueen and Dustin Hoffman. It is the story of a man's struggle for freedom, which is, of course, the ultimate story of mankind. Anyway, without getting too deep into the philosophy of life, I wanted to share with you how the prisoner Papillon, and his fellow criminals, end up on a deserted island for the rest of their lives. On the island they have a pleasant enough existence. Each man has a home to call his own. They have their own chickens and their own plot of land to grow vegetables, and for Dustin Hoffman's character, this is enough. He has already lost his passion for life, along with much of his mind. He is resigned to living out the rest of his days as a prisoner.

However, the character Papillon, played by Steve McQueen, still hungers for his freedom and he knows that the only way to freedom is to jump into the sea. He takes the action, but not before doing his research and putting a plan together. Every day for weeks he takes small actions towards his goal

PART 2: TAKING ACTION!

of freedom. He watches the movement of the waves for hours each day, so that he can calculate which wave will carry him out beyond the jagged rock edges.

He prepares and tests a sturdy raft that will support his weight and still stay buoyant. And when there is nothing more to do in preparation, he jumps. It's a brave man who jumps into a turbulent sea with no guarantee that he will not be killed, or caught, but he manages the fear by considering all the risks, planning his strategy and staying focused on his ultimate goal to become a free man.

> *Taking action is the only thing that will really make the difference. Resolve now to become an action taker. Commit now to taking the first step and in taking the action, you will become the person you are destined to be.*

Mandy called me up, asking for help to find £5,000. She needed it to be able to settle an outstanding bill, and the deadline for payment was at the end of that day. I asked her to come up with three ways that she could find the money. They included asking her daughter to lend it to her, selling her car and asking a friend to repay a loan earlier than agreed. The last option was the most scary for her. However, she was totally committed to having £5,000 by the end of the day, so she took the action that scared her the most.

Now the interesting thing about this real story, and many others that I've witnessed like it, is that the result didn't come from doing the 'right' thing. Mandy's friend didn't repay her the money when she asked her to on that day. The money came in from a completely different source, but it came from Mandy being 100% committed to getting the money. When you are 100% committed you can achieve anything in your life. You can manifest as much money as you like.

How do you know when someone is 100% committed to something? Here are some of the signs...

- They don't mind what others think.

- They are not afraid to ask for help.

- They are not afraid to look stupid.

- They are really afraid of lots of things, but take action anyway.

- They are focused on the end result, rather than the fear.

- They believe that it's possible, even if they don't know how.

- They believe in themselves.

- They trust that everything is happening perfectly.

Only one of the above statements is *proof* of commitment. You might say that you are committed to losing weight, for example, but you cannot resist your mother's home-made cake. That tells me that you are not 100% committed. Or you might say that you are committed to having more money for yourself, but if you continue to spend more than you earn, then you are not 100% committed. If you say you are committed to changing your life but never invest in a coach or a course that will help you to see a new way to live, you are probably not 100% committed to changing things after all.

Your actions tell you more about what you are committed to than your words.

Look at the actions that currently make up an average day for you, and you will see what you are committed to in your life. You may be committed to being busy, to looking good, or to being loved. You may be committed to being comfortable, keeping the peace or staying safe. What activities are you committed to? Is it time with the family or time with the TV soap characters? Is it time with the celebrity gossip or is it time attending a class to learn something new and to meet new people? Is it time spent watching TV talent shows or time spent making your own dreams come true?

You demonstrate your value best by taking actions that are consistent with the actions of someone who values themself and their desires.

Money Magnet Mindset Tool: Committing Yourself to Having More Money

Ask yourself: 'What actions am I taking on a regular basis that show I am 100% committed to having more money?' These are the actions that reinforce a belief in yourself that you are 100% committed and therefore on track to actually have more money. List yours here:

Jumping Out of Your Comfort Zone

Every year there are events held all over the world where you can meet and learn from experts on how to make lots of money by doing what you love. There is no shortage of information, or resources to support you. However, every year I also witness the type of person who sits on the edge, unwilling to commit to anything. They are the ones who are eager to show up and they take copious notes, but at the point when they are asked to commit to a particular course of action, you will find them making for the exit doors, usually muttering something about it being 'all about sales'.

It is a relatively small number who actually commit to taking the steps to become a millionaire. Instead, most people come up with all the reasons why they can't possibly take the next step. They say: 'I can't afford a mentor right now', or 'I don't know what I want to do' or 'I haven't got the time!' It would be much more honest if they were simply to admit that either they don't really want £1million or they are absolutely terrified of jumping out of their comfort zone!

Geeta approached me after hearing me talk at a Millionaire Bootcamp. It had taken her two whole days to build up the courage to approach me, and then to choose to invest in a year-long coaching programme. She did it because she was committed to having more for herself. At the end of that year, Geeta had achieved all her financial goals and so much more. She had become a person of high net worth in every way. The following year I played two short videos of Geeta that showed how she had transformed over the year. She had become a wealthy woman in every aspect by taking actions that were beyond the person that she thought she was, and beyond her own perceived capabilities. It had all started with her having the courage to overcome her fear and to take the first committed step.

When you are crystal clear about what you want, you will have the courage to act on your dreams. If you are not 100% clear, it is when you act that you will find your courage.

◾ Case Study: Looking Beyond Your Fears

Saj called me before a Money Magnet workshop to share that her family disapproved of her attending it, that she had needed to borrow the money to come, and that she was now facing her biggest fears of driving alone on the motorway and talking to a group of strangers. She was really scared, but her commitment to turn her circumstances around was so much bigger than her fear.

Saj was one of the first people to arrive, and just a few hours later we all witnessed the incredible transformation of someone who was scared to speak into a powerful woman who was not afraid to declare what she wanted from life. By taking actions in the face of her fears, Saj fulfilled on her commitment to herself.

At the end of the workshop, Saj declared to me that she was going to hire me as a coach, but that it would take her two weeks to attract the necessary £3,000. At that point she had no idea how she was going do this. She went home and did her accounts. She cleared her clutter and organized her paperwork, and in doing so, within two days she had found the first £400. Two weeks later, she was ready to start the coaching: she had magically attracted the money from work, as an unexpected bonus.

Three months later, Saj had transformed her life. She had found a new job, taken on some private clients, and started a group to help build the confidence of women in her community. She had also transformed her relationship with her husband and become pregnant with her fifth child. The last thing I heard was that she was putting an offer in on a £1.3million house!

You too can have your dream life and as much money as you desire. However, all the affirmations and vision boards in the world won't work unless you take the necessary actions. You must transform your unconscious thoughts and align them to what you really want by taking the actions that are consistent with what you really want.

Money Magnet Mindset Tool: Acting on Your Dreams

If you want to have more money, what do you know that you need to do to get started? Write it down now and schedule when you are going to take this action*.

....

....

....

(*I suggest that you take the action as soon as possible, ideally before the end of today.)

Remember, money is a means of exchanging value. Look for ways in which you can give more of yourself, and offer more value to others, and you will attract people who value you and your offering. Saj started her Confidence Class for Women because she wanted to share what she had learnt. It meant overcoming her fear of speaking out, week after week, and in doing so she became a confident woman herself.

If you want to have more money, look at ways that you can help others to have more money.

Looking for more ways to offer value can be seen as looking at more ways to expand, honour, and grow yourself as a person. The more you honour who you are and what you do, the more others will honour and value you. If you want a pay rise, look at how you can add more value at work. If you want more clients, ask your existing clients what more they would like you to offer them. Give more and the natural laws of the universe will ensure that you receive more in return, directly or indirectly. And you do need to be prepared to jump out of your comfort zone!

Jumping Out of My Comfort Zone

There is a first time for everything, and I remember well the first time I spoke to 500 women at a Millionaire Bootcamp in London. I'd emailed the organizer to request a speaking slot, but when I found out exactly what was involved, the fear kicked in. I didn't respond to the organizers' email when it came in, and it was just ten days before the event that I took the call to confirm my slot.

Now that I was 100% committed, I sprang into action and did everything I had to do to make it a success. When I spoke that afternoon, it was everything I'd ever dreamt of and more. There were queues of women lining up afterwards to speak to me, and to share how I had inspired them to see themselves and their lives in a more powerful way. I knew that I'd made a real difference to a lot of women that day, and the tears in some of their eyes showed me how they had been physically moved by my talk.

There was just one thing – I'd given everything I had, but I hadn't made a single sale!

The next morning I was at breakfast in the hotel when one of the organizers approached me to ask a favour. The opening speaker for that day was missing, so could I prepare a brand new one-hour presentation and be on stage within just 20 minutes? Of course I said *'yes'*, and soon I was miked-up to go back on stage and to reconnect with this gorgeous audience. The difference was that now I knew what it felt like to be on that stage, I was more comfortable and confident in my delivery, and in once again giving everything I had, this time I generated a lot of sales from the event.

I was now going to be able to provide ongoing support to a number of these women, rather than just a moment of inspiration, and in time, many of them have gone on to become inspiring role models for other women, as well as to their own families.

I tell this story to show that we all get scared before doing something that we've never done before. It's normal. It's probably normal too for most people to give in to the fear, and not take any action. I made the initial phone call when I felt lit up and inspired by the possibility of speaking at the event. It was that simple idea translated into action that started the path of fate that enabled me to make a real difference, and to follow my dream of becoming a world-class inspirational speaker.

> *'Inaction breeds doubt and fear. Action breeds confidence and courage. If you want to conquer fear, do not sit home and think about it. Go out and get busy.'*
> **– Dale Carnegie**

The other point worth noting is that I didn't get hung up on the lack of sales on the first day. I knew that I had given my best, and that I had made a difference, so there was no room for disappointment.

> *When you know that you have given great value, you will have such a good feeling inside that you don't need any external validation.*

When you acknowledge yourself for stepping up and becoming more than you thought you were capable of, the Law of Attraction determines that 'like attracts like' and you will receive more in return. It is guaranteed: just as the law of gravity dictates that a ball will fall downwards if dropped.

Overcoming Your Fears

The thing that 'scares' me the most these days is technology. I don't understand it. However, when I looked at how I could help as many people as possible through speaking, I realized that one of the answers was to deliver weekly webinars.

Now the idea of using technology to connect with people that I couldn't even see was really challenging, and my very first webinar was a total disaster! I spoke for a whole hour before I realized that my mike wasn't working! My biggest fear, of letting people down, had happened... but I was still alive and they all came back the next week.

The more webinars I hosted, the better I got at understanding the technology and the techniques needed to deliver the best results. I was able to invite guest speakers to join me and to provide live coaching to anyone in the world. I kept looking for more ways to add value and the number of people signing up to the webinars increased. As I help others to make more money, I make more money for myself too.

The main thing is to get started and to take some action right now on an idea that inspires you. It could be anything from making a phone call to organizing a family get-together. It could be starting that new exercise regime or calling a prospective client. It could be organizing a charity fundraiser, starting a new business or launching a new product. Whatever it is, get started now! Go for it!

What scares you today will be part of your skill set tomorrow.

Now is the time. This is why you are reading this book right now. Now is the time to commit to what you know in your heart you want to do – no matter how scary it may feel. If you're not sure what you want to do, just pick one thing right now to focus on and the rest will unfold perfectly. Sometimes it is only when you take action in one direction that you get clear on which direction you really want to be taking, as in the following example.

■ Case study: Trust Your Gut Feeling

Andrew Sage had been made redundant, once again. Since graduating with a computer science degree, he had experienced business failure on more than one occasion. Along the way he had run up a sizeable credit card debt from living as if he were still employed when he no longer had a job.

Andrew asked himself the following questions: 'What is it that I really want to do?', 'What is it that ignites my spark? and 'What is it that makes me want to get up in the morning?' When he took the time to listen to and trust himself, what he came up with was a card game he'd invented called Symbotica.

Now some may say that Andrew was mad to focus all his time and energy on his card game. Wouldn't it be wiser to just get another job? But Andrew knew from experience that jobs held no guarantee, and so he decided instead to trust his gut feeling and focus on selling and promoting Symbotica. In fact, you'll find Andrew if you look for SymboticaAndrew on Twitter.

What happened next is a perfect example of how life can unfold once you focus on your heart's desire and let go of how you will achieve your success. Andrew approached me and Rachel Elnaugh with his Symbotica card game, and then the three of us created an app called 'Nine Star Ki' as a quick way for people to consult Nine Star Ki astrology.

Andrew started to become known as someone who could create apps easily. He created the Heart's Desire app, and then the Water app, which reminds users to drink water during the day. More followed, and all of his apps were joint-venture opportunities that sprung out of his being committed to his dream, and taking the actions necessary to promote his card game. While following his passion and helping others, Andrew magically attracted to himself a contract opportunity worth £80,000, which was more than enough to settle any outstanding debt he had. Andrew is now loving his life, living it to the full, and offering immense value from doing what he loves to do best!

'It is literally true that you can succeed best and quickest by helping others to succeed.'
– **Napoleon Hill**

Sharing Your Value with Others

If you have something of value to offer, you need to be able to stand up and share it with others, and yet many people are scared of public speaking. Their fear will stop them from taking the action that could transform their business or career overnight.

When people ask me how they can overcome their fear of public speaking, I have the following suggestions:

1.   Prepare well.

2.   Be clear on the value you are offering.

3.   Put aside all preparations once you are in front of the audience.

4.   Be there for your audience.

Following these steps means that as soon as you are on that stage, you have to give up *thinking* about yourself and focus on *giving* as much of yourself to the people in the room. In that space of giving, there is no fear, and it's only when you take those actions that you'll discover the secret for yourself!

MONEY MAGNET MINDSET HABITS: 'AN ACTION A DAY KEEPS THE FEAR AWAY!'

- Every day, take one action that scares you.

- When you think you're finished for the day, make one extra phone call.

- Keep looking to see how you can provide more value to others.

- Commit to swapping one hour of TV for one hour that adds value to your work.

- Schedule tasks aligned with your biggest goals, no matter how small the task.

- Learn how to master something that you don't know how to do right now.

- Become an action taker and take on additional projects if they inspire you.

- Resist looking at your belly button and focus on what you can provide for others.

- Say 'no' to someone at least once a week.

- Say 'yes' every day to the life that you have chosen!

PART 3

BELIEF

'If I have the belief that I can do it, I shall surely acquire the capacity to do it even if I may not have it at the beginning.'

Mahatma Gandhi

PART 3

BELIEF

Chapter 8

Uncover Your True Value

'I find the less you focus on your flaws, the better off you are. Be yourself and be glad of who you are.'
– **Michelle Pfeiffer**

Congratulations on getting to this point – particularly if you have done the work and taken the actions in Parts 1 and 2 to get here.

The thing is, it's a bit of a chicken-and-egg situation. In this section I'm going to give you lots of extra tools and techniques that will build up your sense of self-worth. However, in my experience, the only thing that is guaranteed to increase your personal value is you taking the actions that up until now you have been avoiding.

That is why this book is structured in the way it is: first you need to focus 100% on what you really want, and then you need to take lots of inspired actions that will stretch how you perceive yourself, and it is at this point that you will start to value yourself more. On the other hand, I have met lots of people who know what they want to do, and even how to go about doing it, and yet the image they have of themselves is getting in their way on some level. They just don't see themselves as achieving all their dreams.

Maybe someone told *you* that you'd never be good enough to do something, or that you can't have everything you want... and you believed them. You may only have been young at the time, but if a belief like that launches itself into your unconscious mind, can you see how it's going to get in the way every time it looks like you might just succeed?

■ Case Study: If You Think You're Great, Others Will Think You're Great!

Helen came along to a Money Magnet workshop, but she was so late that she missed the whole morning! She then joined the Money Magnet Mastermind Group and was late again for the first session. Helen was very keen, and willing to work harder than anyone else, but she had been struggling to make her business succeed.

I explained to Helen that each member of the group had been painting a vision to represent what they wanted from the course. I asked her if she could draw out her vision, too. *'Oh no!'* she exclaimed, *'I'm rubbish at art!'* There was something in the way she said this that made me want to explore further.

Helen explained that when she was 12 years old, her art teacher had told the whole class that *'Helen is rubbish at art'*. In that moment she felt a strong emotion of shame and humiliation, and she determined that nobody was ever going to call her 'rubbish' again. She then spent her life proving to everyone, including herself, that she wasn't rubbish, and in doing so she ended up behaving like someone who 'knew' inside that she *was* rubbish! The thing is that she never was and never will be 'rubbish', unless, of course, she chooses to believe that about herself.

All the time that Helen had believed this to be true of herself, she had inadvertently been sending out the wrong message to people. This explained why, despite being 100% committed to her coaching business, people were always finding reasons not to buy from her, and she was struggling to find clients. She was also struggling financially.

Taking action wasn't enough for Helen. She had to clear this debilitating unconscious belief about herself before she could be successful. Otherwise, for her, taking action would be like filling a bucket that had a hole in its bottom! She had to realize that what she believed to be a truth about herself was actually completely made up.

Even if she hadn't been very good at art at that age, it didn't mean that she couldn't be good at art now, and it certainly never meant that she was rubbish! Fortunately, as soon as Helen realized the absurdity of her belief, she dumped it for a new, much more empowering belief. She chose to become a Money Magnet, and by the end of the year she had written and published her own book called *Gorgeous Inside and Out,* and successfully launched The Manchester Coaching Academy.

Money Magnet Mindset Tool: Clean Up the Lies You're Telling Yourself

What were you told as a child? Tick the statements below that resonate most with you.*

You're a naughty girl/boy.

You can't have everything you want.

You can't have it all.

Don't be greedy.

You need to share with others.

Children should be seen and not heard.

You can only have it when you've eaten everything on your plate.

Good girl/boy for finishing your plate.

Be nice to them.

Give them your sweeties.

Children do as they're told.

Be quiet or I'll make you be quiet.

It's rude to ask for what you want.

It's rude to help yourself.

Only good girls and boys get presents from Father Christmas.

Just behave yourself!

When will you ever learn?

*If you're a parent, please don't panic about what you may have told your children, and the impact it could have on them. Naturally we need to be responsible about the messages we are giving our children, but I promise you that you cannot control how what you say will be taken on board. It is part of human nature for us to interpret things differently, and to create our own version of the world. Just as one person will see snow and smile as they remember happy times, another will see snow and grimace, remembering the time their car got stuck in it. It's just snow.

Is that voice still inside your head? Is that what's been holding you back? Can you see that it's a bit out of date now? Can you see that it doesn't have to be a command that you must follow for the rest of your life? Instead, you can make up a new command, like: 'You can now have everything you've always wanted because you are worth it', or 'You are always the perfect you, whatever you do, because there is only ever one of you!'

We do the same thing with the word 'money'. One person will associate greed and nastiness with the word and another will think of joy and the difference that money can make in the world. It simply depends on their experiences and what they made it all mean. Money is simply energy, with no personality of its own.

Are You Resisting Wealth?

Back to you and how you perceive yourself – and your relationship with money and self-worth. If you have bought into the idea, at least on some level, that you can't have it all, or that you'll never be good enough, you will be energetically deterring people from buying from you, or awarding you a pay rise.

I remember a personal trainer on one of the Money Magnet workshops who realized there and then how she had been actively putting customers off buying from her. I'd called her up and shared how I desperately needed to lose some weight, and how I needed somebody like her to take me in hand. I practically begged her to be my personal trainer! Her response was that she was still working on her different pricing packages, and that we were about to go into the holiday season so it wasn't worth starting now. She'd get back to me in six weeks' time. But I wanted to lose the weight *before* the holiday season!!

Understanding that she was pushing her customers away didn't help; she needed to take action. She needed to create her pricing packages, and most of all she had to say: 'Yes Marie-Claire, I can help you, and I'd like you to be my client.' She had to accept her true value and how much difference she could make to me: 'Marie-Claire, I can help you to become the person you want to become.' Only when she was clear that what she offered was worth every penny of the price she was charging, could she authentically ask me for the money: 'Marie-Claire, I recommend that you take the monthly payment plan of... and

that will have you wearing your tight jeans again in no time!'
Big smile!

Having spent over 20 years coaching salespeople, I can tell you
that there are three requisite beliefs you must hold if you want
to convince someone else to buy from you:

1. Belief in what you're doing.

2. Belief in the product or service you are offering.

3. Belief in yourself.

This is why it is crucial that you follow your dream and do
what you really want to do with your life. Doing a job just to
earn money will not last long. Think how you might feel about
buying from a salesperson who is only interested in taking
your money and hitting their own sales target. I suspect that
you wouldn't be very keen to buy from somebody with that
mindset. Even as a highly skilled salesperson, if you don't
believe in what you're doing or in what you're selling, how
fulfilled will you be at the end of the day?

I have met successful salespeople on Money Magnet workshops
who are earning lots of money and who still feel poor. This is
because they are not valuing what they do, and so they can't
value the money they receive from doing it. They are often
spending their money on everyone but themselves because,
ultimately, they don't value themselves. They are not paying
attention to their inner voice.

How can you value someone who isn't valuing themselves
and taking the actions to show that they value themselves? It

would be like trying to pay a compliment to someone who kept pushing you away with a negative response. The good news is that in recognizing that they want more for themselves and in taking the action to invest in the workshop, they realize how great they are, and start to attract more wealth as a result. Ultimately, you have to care enough about yourself to invest your time in reading a book like this, getting on a workshop, or starting your own business.

> *The only person who can know how you feel about you is you. The only person who has the power to increase your value is you. When you accept that you are worth more, you will effortlessly attract more into your life.*

What Antenna Message are You Projecting?

We saw earlier how Helen's deprecating self-talk was pushing people away from buying from her. Remember, we are all energetic beings and we are all connected energetically. You can feel it when somebody isn't 100% with you, and when someone is feeling out of sorts. People were picking up Helen's antenna message without always being consciously aware of it. They probably couldn't logically explain why they didn't want to take on a coach right there and then – maybe it wasn't the right time for them or maybe they didn't have enough money (that old excuse!) The truth was that they had picked up from Helen that it would be wise not to buy from her. After all, she was sending out the message that she was rubbish!

So, you need to dump any negative self-talk. There's no point in spending a fortune on marketing and advertising your business if its biggest advert – you – is sending out the wrong message. Are you starting to see the huge impact that your thoughts have on your life? Especially your thoughts about yourself.

Money Magnet Mindset Tool: Commanding Your Mind

Let's start by translating all those earlier negative commands into more positive ones. Your unconscious loves commands. It only knows how to obey, so let's start making use of the best tool in your toolkit: your own mind!

Negative Command	Positive Command
You're a naughty girl/boy.	You're free to do what you want to do.
Be a good girl/boy.	You're really good at being you.
You can't have everything you want.	You already have everything you want!
Don't be greedy.	You deserve to feel special.
You need to share with others.	There is plenty for everyone.
Children should be seen and not heard.	Speak up!
Good girl/boy for finishing your plate.	Complete things.
Be nice to them.	Be nice to yourself.

continued on p.186

continued from p.185

Negative Command	Positive Command
Give them your sweeties.	Give yourself some money.
Children do as they're told.	Do what you know is right.
Be quiet or I'll make you be quiet.	Be still within.
It's rude to ask for what you want.	Ask for what you want.
It's rude to help yourself.	Ask for help if you need it.
Do as you're told!	Do unto others as you would have done to you.
Only good girls and boys get presents.	God always provides.
Just behave yourself!	Just be yourself!
When will you ever learn?	Keep learning.

The positive commands above are just to get you started. I'm sure you can make up a few of your own. If you've been listening to the old negative commands for most of your life, you need to start training your mind to accept some positive ones.

Retraining Your Mind to Accept New Commands

When your mind receives new information, it checks it with past information received. For example, if you get lucky on the lottery, it will check to see if this has happened before. If it finds little evidence that it has happened before, it may conclude that you 'never win lottery prizes', and you may even find yourself responding to a lucky win with the words, 'Who, me? I never win anything!'

Now with those words, you have just reinforced the belief that you are not a lucky person who wins prizes, and if anyone is listening, you have invited them to believe that about you too! Next time you win a prize, your brain will search for a similar occurrence. It may find the earlier win, but the overriding sense will be one of 'not winning anything' because that was what was reinforced in the moment, and what was made real through your words. The likelihood is that you'll never win much, and anything you do win you'll probably lose, just so that you can reinforce the idea that 'you never win anything!'

To retrain your mind to be aligned with a more positive image of yourself and your life, you need to start collecting evidence to support the new belief. It is only when the evidence of a new belief outweighs that of the old belief that you will have recreated yourself as you wish to be. It will take some discipline and practice, so you really do have to want to change things. However, I guess that if you've taken all the actions in the book up to this point, you are already committed, and you will already have lots of new evidence to support your dreams.

You're Free to Do What You Want to Do

It's your life. Nobody else can live it for you. When you're on your deathbed, what will you wish that you'd done? What are you not doing because somebody said you couldn't?

I recently watched a TV programme about a woman who wasn't good with her money and who wasn't valuing herself and her dreams. The researchers uncovered that she had always wanted to sing, but instead of choosing to further a career in singing, she'd sidestepped her dreams and opted to direct performances rather than be in them. The answer in her case was to start taking singing lessons and to honour the part of her that wanted to sing. By booking herself in for the singing classes, she showed in her actions that she now valued herself more. By honouring her own desires, including that of wanting more money, she was then able rapidly to turn around her finances.

Write down now what you are going to do for yourself, and by when:

....

....

Date..

You're Really Good at Being You

Do you fall into the trap of comparing yourself with others? You may be doing really well and feeling really good about yourself and then you see someone whom you judge to be better than you. At that moment all the good feelings that you had about yourself vanish, and you recreate yourself as a 'never-be-good-enough' version of the real you. Can you see how crazy that is?

No one can possibly be a better you than you.

If you are in the habit of comparing yourself with others, I recommend that you use the technique of 'mirrors' to create a more positive outcome. The principle of mirrors is that you will energetically attract people who are mirrors of yourself. These are people who are showing up in your life to reflect back to you the qualities you are refusing to acknowledge in yourself. Start acknowledging their positive qualities as evidence that you have the same positive qualities.

It took me years before I could finally accept that I was beautiful. Using the mirror technique meant that, after a while, it was impossible for me to deny my beauty when I was surrounded by beautiful people everywhere I went!

Write down the positive qualities of the people in your life whom you currently judge to be better than you:

....

....

....

....

....

Look at this list every day until you can accept these qualities in yourself.

You Already Have Everything You Want!

We established in Chapter 1 that you create your own reality. It is time to accept that everything in your life is there because, on some level, you wanted it there. Now you can either be right about the fact that you didn't want your debts or your illness or your job, or you can start to look at why you might have chosen it. This will give you a lot more power.

Patrick complained that he was getting headaches; his head felt all messed up. He had fallen out with his wife, and while he knew that he needed to have a conversation about money with her, he couldn't all the time he was getting these headaches. I suggested that he was using the headaches as an excuse and asked him what he was really afraid of. Patrick saw that he was afraid of getting clear about what he wanted because then he would have to face his fear of asking for what he wanted! He'd chosen confusion over clarity. Once he took an action to commit to what he wanted, his head cleared.

Money Magnet Tool: You Can Have it All!

Write down everything that doesn't work in your life right now.
(For example: 'I'm single and I want to be married', or 'I'm poor and I want to be rich.')

....
....
....
....

Think about and then write down *why* you have chosen this for yourself.
(For example: 'I'm single because I love doing what I want *when* I want', or 'I'm poor because I prefer to spend time with my family rather than working.')

....
....
....
....

Now write down what you want and why you think you can't have it. Then add the word 'and' to create what you want from what you already have.

(For example: 'I can do what I want *and* be married!' or 'I can spend time with my family *and* be rich.') Now you have a new, more powerful affirmation that is aligned with what you really want! Try it for yourself:

....

....

....

....

You Deserve to Feel Special

What are you doing to make other people feel special? Do you pay compliments or buy spontaneous gifts for loved ones? Do you create a world around you where everyone feels special? Most importantly, are you acknowledging the compliments that others are paying you?

If you don't give freely and lovingly, you will find it more difficult to receive. If there is always an 'in order to' behind your giving, you will be suspicious of anyone who makes you feel special, including yourself!

Acknowledge that you are special and that the world would be a poorer place without you in it. Take three deep breaths and feel yourself connected to the Earth. Feel yourself to be as much a part of the universe as the most beautiful flower or the shining stars in the sky. Smile, because you know that you're a special as they are!

There is Plenty for Everyone

If all the wealth in the world today was apportioned equally, there would be more than enough money for everyone. Always share a percentage of your income with those who have no resources to create their own. Giving it to charity (or tithing, as it is often called) is an excellent way to affirm your wealth. However, do not give away what you don't have. Create more value and more money will come. When you have enough money, show others the formula that you have used and you will always be rich. Give others the tools, rather than the money, just as Jo Luck of Heifer International did with Tererai in Zimbabwe (see Chapter 5).

Entrepreneurs should be acknowledged and praised for creating wealth from nothing but their own wits and creativity. A few years ago I met an incredible entrepreneur who had used his financial skills to create his own mortgage company employing over 700 people and their families. It was a great success.

However, when hard times hit he was forced to close the company, and for two years he was racked with guilt about how he had let down all those people. He then came back by looking at how he could help struggling families hold on to their homes during hard times. He used his knowledge of the mortgage industry to find the necessary loopholes, and people who really wanted to keep their homes would always find the money to pay him on a 'no win, no fee' basis.

It's curious how people will always find money they need if they really, really want something enough – whether it's cigarettes, a holiday, or to live in their own home. There is enough money for everyone. Some people just may not want it as much as others, or are simply not looking at how they could offer more to the world around them.

Think of the last time that you wanted something so badly that you found a way to find the money. Write it down here:

....

....

Acknowledge how creative you are as a human being. Embrace that creativity and write down how you could help others in a way that they would value enough to want to pay you money for your product or service.

....

....

Speak Up!

If you have an idea, honour it. If you have something important to say, say it. Don't live your life thinking, 'What if?' or 'What will people think?' Anyone in the Mind, Body and Spirit field will explain to you that your creativity is channelled through your throat. An idea in your head will never amount to anything until you speak it into existence.

You cannot perceive the value of your idea until you ask someone else to put a price on it. When you stay silent you deprive the world of your full value. When you deny your truth, you stop believing in yourself, and by now you will know what comes next – when you don't believe in yourself, no one else will believe in you.

Jack was a well-spoken and well-educated young man who was training to be a lawyer. His father was in the legal profession and it had always been expected that Jack would become a lawyer too. The thing was, Jack was starting to realize that he didn't want to be a lawyer. He wanted to be in theatre. It was only when he had the courage to speak out and tell his family that he was ditching law to become an actor that he could finally fully accept and trust himself. When he honoured his truth, everyone around him respected his decision too.

I remember when I took the decision to turn my back on the corporate job with the big salary, company car and fat expense account. I knew that it was the right thing for me to do, and I was inundated with lunch invitations from people who wanted to know how I could walk away from the money. What they didn't understand is this:

Money follows you once you embrace and honour your full value.

Where is it that you are not speaking up or telling the truth? Are you asking for your going rate? Are you avoiding having any conversation about money? Are you doing the whole sales pitch and then dreading the bit when the customer asks your price?

Identify what it is that you need to say. Write it out here and take the time to practise saying it to the person in the mirror.

Continue until the person in the mirror agrees with you, or says 'yes!'

....

....

Complete Things

Have you ever met someone who keeps saying that they're going to write a book or start a business? Maybe *you* have been saying for a while you're going to get around to doing something? It's exhausting, isn't it? Compare that to the feeling you get when you sit down and deal with what needs doing – whether it's writing a book, starting a new business, completing a tax return or just a phone call that you need to make. Just starting the task feels good, and completing it can make you feel nothing less than heroic!

Recall the last time that you completed something and how good it felt. Think of a few times when you completed what needed doing, and jot them down now. Examples could include passing your driving test, writing an essay or a blog, cooking a dish, returning a phone call, filling out a form, paying your bills, doing your accounts or finishing a book.

....

....

....

Start collecting evidence of yourself as a 'completer'. It feels good doesn't it?

Be Nice to Yourself

You're always being told to be nice to others, and to give to others. It feels great to give. It feels great to be nice, and it's also good to receive and to be nice to yourself. I meet a lot of people who can't stop giving and giving, and then they complain that they don't have enough money, or that it's not fair that others have more than they do. You need to start looking after yourself if you want to have plenty to give to others, whether it's energy, money or love.

What is it that you give out most to others? Is it money, gifts, compliments or coaching? Is it help around the house, healing or therapy, or simply your time? Whatever it is, look to see where you need to give *yourself* more of this. Write down what you will do differently from now on in order to be nicer to yourself.

....

....

....

....

Do What You Know is Right

As a child, you are generally expected to do as you are told by your parents or carers. It makes sense, and it prevents you from burning your hand on a hot stove or running out into the path of an oncoming car. Adults make great teachers while you're growing up, but there comes a point when you know what you need to know to survive and you can start to make your own choices. Am I stating the obvious? Maybe, but I bet you still have your parents' voices in your head from time to time, drowning out your own clear voice!

Write down here, or in your notebook, some of the choices you are currently facing. Note down what choice you would make if you were listening to your parents; what choice you would make if you were defying them; and finally, what choice you would *like* to make.

....

....

....

....

Practise making your own choices and taking responsibility when they work out, as well as when things don't work out as expected. If it is always your authentic choice, you know that it will always be the right choice, and, however things look right now, it will always turn out to be the perfect choice.

Be Still Within

There is a quiet place within you where you will always find peace. You can go there whenever you like, to recharge your batteries. It took me years to find this place. I was too busy talking and using up every minute being busy! Then I found that I could be more productive by slowing down, listening to others, and even taking time out of my busy schedule to do nothing. Before, I was coming from a place of scarcity, where there was never enough time or money or love. Finding this place of acceptance and serenity is like finding a lake in the baking hot sands of a desert.

Discover your wealth within, and keep it with you at all times if you can. Find a place where you can sit quietly and uninterrupted each day. Set aside your thoughts about your day and allow yourself to relax into a deep meditative state. You may wish to keep a piece of paper handy to note down any inspiration that comes from being in this still space. After doing this regularly, you'll find it much easier to tap into your stillness, even in the midst of a busy day or a conversation. Enjoy!

Ask For What You Want

It's amazing how many of us have learnt the art of saying everything except what it is that we really want! I want you to know that it's okay to ask for what you want. If it's what you really want, it probably won't be as much of a surprise to the people you're asking as you may think.

Sophie was a hard worker who hadn't had a pay rise for a few years. She decided that she deserved a pay rise and so she asked her boss for one. When she received notification of a 2.5% pay rise, Sophie went back and asked for more. She was then delighted to receive a pay rise of no less than 20% during what many would describe as tough economic times. Even more interestingly, when she bumped into the owner of the business a couple of weeks later, he congratulated her on her pay rise and apologized that it hadn't been awarded a lot sooner!

What are *you* going to ask for? Write down what you want, *who* you're going to ask, and *when* you're going to pop the question.

....

....

....

Ask for Help if You Need It

If you learnt to be self-sufficient at an early age, asking for help may seem like a sign of weakness. To be coached or mentored you have to be prepared to open up and talk about some of your deepest secrets, and if you've spent all your life pretending to the world that you're okay, that's going to be a challenge for you. However, it is the most amazing opportunity to trust another human being and, as we are all connected, it is one of the best ways to demonstrate that you can trust yourself.

Trust yourself to make the perfect choice of team to support you, and allow yourself to be authentic in all your relationships. When everyone in the world starts to honour who they really are, and follow their intuitive path, we will connect together perfectly, as in the rest of nature, and the exchange of value will be effortless.

Ask someone today for help, no matter how small the task, and receive their response graciously and with love.

Do Unto Others as You Would Have Done to You

As a child you were told what to do. As an adult you have to decide what is right and what is wrong. The world is changing, so some of what you learnt as a child may no longer be good advice. The best rule of thumb is to adopt the principle of doing unto others as you would have done to you.

You are going to have to stay alert to your thoughts and judgements about others, and to be prepared to change those unloving thoughts in an instant. Davina MacKail, the Dream Whisperer, talks of how she struggles with staying in that space when she finds herself in a queue. Her magic tip is to use an 'inner smile' to transform that moment into one of love.

Try using an 'inner smile' when you spot yourself resisting being with other people.

God Always Provides

One of the problems with buying into the notion that 'only good girls and boys get presents' is that a lot of us, when we were children, were told that we were 'bad' for not finishing our food, or not doing our homework, and so on.

It is time to accept that you are always provided for in this world. Just as the sun comes up every morning and clouds will lead to rain, the universe will always provide. There are always enough nuts for the squirrels and grain for the birds, but they do have to make an effort to get it! You can't imagine nuts flying to the squirrel that's sitting on its perch wanting to be a 'nut magnet!' No, the squirrel would starve if it didn't go searching for its food. In the same way, you need to use what God gave you to go find the money that is always available to you.

There is an abundance of money available to you. All you need to do is to find your way to harvest it.

Close your eyes and take three deep breaths. Understand that all the money you want is available to you right now. You have the combination numbers to the lock. Now all you need to do is tap into the inspiration, write down the ideas you receive, and take immediate action!

Just Be Yourself!

If the daffodil tried to be a rose, it would be weird, wouldn't it? And yet so many of us look to copy others rather than accept the authentic and rich value of ourselves.

Write down what you would do if you had permission to be totally yourself, and could choose to do whatever you wanted:

....

....

....

Keep Learning

It's a fallacy that when we've completed our education, we are complete as human beings. The truth is that we renew ourselves daily, and we physically recreate the cells in our whole body every seven years. You are not the same person as you were seven years ago: you are the sum of all your experiences and learnings. Now that you know yourself to be a creator, and responsible for the world around you, does that not invite you to want to learn as much as possible about who you are, and what you might be capable of?

What new skill would you like to master? Write it down and commit *now* to registering on a course, or finding a mentor to instruct you in that skill.

....

....

....

You Are Amazing!

If you were told off a lot as a child, you may have developed your own internal 'telling off' voice. You know, the one that is constantly belittling what you do and making sure that no one can hurt you because you've already done the worst damage! Well, it's time to give it the boot!

Instead, I want you to meet the person inside you who is always so proud of you and your accomplishments. This person always sees the positive. They see that you have done your best, whatever the outcome, and they acknowledge you every day. They see only your beauty, your enchanting essence and your energy.

Keep a night-time journal acknowledging at least five things that you have achieved during the day. Read your acknowledgements first thing every morning and whenever you need a boost!

Congratulations on completing this chapter and embracing that you are a natural Money Magnet! (You'd simply forgotten who you really were along the way!)

Chapter 9

Believe in Your Assets

*'Wouldn't it be powerful if you fell in love with
yourself so deeply that you would do just about
anything if you knew it would make you happy?
This is precisely how much life loves you and wants
you to nurture yourself. The deeper you love yourself,
the more the universe will affirm your worth. Then
you can enjoy a lifelong love affair that brings you
the richest fulfilment from inside out.'*
– Alan Cohen

Today could be the start of a brand new love affair with
yourself, so you may wish to mark it in some way.

I remember the day when I realized I'd been running around
looking for love and appreciation from everyone other
than myself. I was 'still single' and I was facing yet another
birthday on my own (can you hear the violins of the 'poor
me' syndrome?). I was tired of wanting to be married so that

I would feel loved and accepted and normal! I resolved right there and then that if nobody else was going to choose to love me, then I might as well be the one to love me!

If you're waiting for someone else to make you rich, I recommend that you give up that idea right now and resolve to make it happen yourself!

I marked my commitment to myself by taking two items from my jewellery box and having them made into my very own engagement ring. It was a symbol of my commitment to love, cherish and obey myself for the rest of my life, and a reminder to demonstrate that love for myself every single day.

Money Magnet Mindset Tool: Your Commitment to Yourself

How are you going to mark your commitment to yourself? You might choose to perform a ritual or a ceremony. You might get a tattoo or choose an item of jewellery. You might have a party for all your friends, just to celebrate the wonder of you and how much you value being you.

Write down how you will celebrate and commemorate your commitment to love, cherish and obey yourself for the rest of your life:

....

....

....

Acknowledging Your Worth in the World

Your birthday is an excuse to stop for a second and celebrate your birth into this world. It is a chance to look at how you enrich the world just by being here, and by being who you are today. Celebrate your birthday. You may even wish to create a second birthday – like the Queen – for the day that you realized your true worth.

If you had any idea of how many people you touch, and how you make a difference just by being you, you would be amazed. Just ask some of the people in your life how you make a difference to them, and be prepared to accept your value as reflected in their eyes and words. When you start to accept your true value, the possibilities are endless.

> *'Too many people overvalue what they are not and undervalue what they are.'*
> – **Malcolm S. Forbes**

Consider that there are roughly 7 billion people in the world today. When you make a difference to just one person a day, and *that* person makes a difference to one person a day, you start to create a viral epidemic of 'making a difference' to the world you live in.

Over a lifetime, using those figures would mean that you being on this Earth adds value to more than 650 million people! (365 days x 70 years = 25,550; then 25,550 x 25,550 = 652,802,500 people). Wow! Let me say that again: You being on this Earth adds value to more than 650 million people!

Even if this year you only made a difference to one person in a whole week (which would mean you being a virtual recluse!), that would be 52 people. And if those 52 people, because of you, then made a difference to just one person a week, that would be 2,704 people. And if those 2,704 people made a difference to 52 people a year, we are already up to 140,608 people that you have indirectly affected just by being you this year.

And if those people then make a difference to just one person a week, this adds up to a total of 7,311,616 people in just one year! Now imagine if the difference made to each of these people was worth just one pound in value. After all, we measure value in money; it is the common denominator. Can you see that you being you, and connecting to other people, makes you worthy of being at least a millionaire? It's time to accept your full worth. Money is an exchange of value.

When you accept your full worth, you will be receptive to attracting more money in return. If I had acknowledged my intrinsic value as a sales director who inspired others to achieve £1million sales each month, I would have been able to *accept* my full reward, instead of spending it as fast as I could.

Once you accept that it is you being true to you that makes that difference, and creates value in the world, I will help you see that you are worthy of millions because you have, by embracing who you really are, the ability to touch millions. All you need to do is honour your true self, stay connected, and open up your heart to receive. You can become a Money Magnet Millionaire.

How Do You Value yourself?

It is not the wedding ceremony that makes a marriage, but the daily commitment to love one another. Instead of focusing on what needs to be fixed about you, why not start appreciating what is already perfect about you and your life.

> *It is not in reading this book that you become a Money Magnet. It is in the actions that you take on a daily basis that you demonstrate your value.*

Just as you love a partner for their good bits and their not-so-good bits, maybe it is time to love and accept yourself in the same way? Commit now to do whatever it takes, for the rest of your life, to honour who you really are and what you really want.

If you understood that your life's mission was to value who you are, just as you are, what would you do differently? How would you demonstrate that love for yourself each and every day? How would you value your body, your mind, your time, your money, your skills and abilities, your environment, and the work and the friends you have chosen?

Value Your Body

Do you love the body you have? How do you demonstrate that love? Do you dress in a way that makes you feel good about yourself? Do you indulge your body in activities that make you feel good? Whether you choose belly dancing, weightlifting, running or salsa dancing, are you celebrating the amazing joy and energy that you have within you?

Mandy was searching for ways to be happy and rich, but she kept looking to others for the answers. When she looked within, she remembered how much she loved to climb mountains. By making a commitment to devote at least one weekend a month to doing what she loved most, she demonstrated how much she valued herself. She then became more powerful in demanding her full value from others.

What activity do you love to do? How do you love and nurture your body? Do you consider your diet, the way you breathe, your choice of exercise and therapy treatments? If you know that you enjoy a massage, and that a weekly massage may cost you £90, budget that into your finances and then look for ways to earn that extra money, because you're worth it.

Too many of us only look after ourselves because we want to look good for others, or to adhere to society's guidelines about what is or isn't acceptable. Why not choose to nurture your body as a demonstration of respect for who you are? If you don't look after your body, the chances are that you will become more susceptible to illness and a lack of energy. Remember, 'Big Energy = Big Money'. In my work, I have found a direct correlation between a person's wealth and their health. The more a person commits to the life and money they want, the more the weight drops off them.

> *'I used to go around looking as frumpy as possible because it was inconceivable you could be attractive as well as be smart. It wasn't until I started being myself, the way I like to turn out to meet people, that I started to get any work.'*
> – **Catherine Zeta-Jones**

You owe it to yourself to be well-groomed, to exercise daily and to follow a healthy diet. Do it because you love to do it. Do it because you value your body. It is one of your most valuable assets, and it will repay the investment you make in it a thousandfold.

Money Magnet Mindset Tool: Valuing Your Body

Note down what you now commit to do as a way of demonstrating how much you value your body:

....

....

....

Value Your Mind

Many years ago, I was a heavy smoker. I had lots of reasons to justify being a smoker, but in my mind I knew that it didn't serve me. The final straw came when I could no longer shut out the thoughts every time I went to smoke a cigarette. I wasn't thinking good thoughts about myself. I was 'beating myself up'. My thoughts were along the lines of, 'You loser!' I saw that I was harming myself, and I didn't want to do that anymore. In honouring what my mind had been telling me all along, I gave up smoking. I chose to value myself more than I valued smoking, and in the end my mind was more powerful than any addiction.

The fact that you are reading this book suggests that you already value the power of your mind to create the life you want for yourself. Your mind is enriched by your life experiences and your mind is capable of enriching your life, so choose wisely how you feed your mind. Make a commitment to avoid gossip or mindless activities. Watching TV is the equivalent of being brainwashed, so choose your programmes wisely! Read books and watch films that move and inspire you, and invest in more knowledge that will only enhance your intrinsic value.

'Invest three per cent of your income in yourself (personal development) in order to guarantee your future.'
– **Brian Tracey**

Your mind is your most valuable asset. Invest in courses and materials that train you to make the most of it. If you want to have more money, learn how to overcome your fears of success, and learn everything there is to know about money. Remember, what the mind can conceive the person can achieve. You can lose all your money, but if you still have your mind, it is easy to make it all again. Value your mind over and above anything that is external to you.

Don't swamp your mind with endless 'to do' lists, fears, or judgements on how you could do better. Keep it clear so that it can create new possibilities for you. Take time out to go for a walk, meditate, or do absolutely nothing. Welcome your intuitive thoughts and act on them: the more you follow your natural intuition, the more you will learn to trust your own mind. If you don't listen to your own mind, you can't expect others to follow your lead in the external world.

'What the mind of man can conceive and believe, it can achieve.'
– **Napoleon Hill**

Nothing is impossible if you can first see it in your mind. The many creations of mankind have all started off in the minds of someone, whether it was Edison, Mozart or Branson. The next great idea could already be germinating in *your* mind. Take the time to clear out the clutter so you can uncover the nectar of inspiration.

Money Magnet Mindset Tool: Clearing Your Mind of Clutter

Empty your mind of all its endless chatter. Write down *absolutely everything* that needs doing. Clear your mind of confusion by talking things through with a friend or a coach, or by writing out the pros and cons of an idea in your journal or notebook.

If in doubt, just take action. Nothing clears the mind better than completing a task. When you start something, you'll find out pretty soon whether it was the right thing to start!

Honour your mind by committing to the ideas and dreams that it cherishes, irrespective of others' beliefs or judgements. That is when you will rediscover yourself and your true value. You need to practise listening and trusting your own mind. Start small by learning to follow your intuition. Intuition is one of our biggest gifts and it is seriously undervalued in Western society.

I remember once having a really vivid dream about winning at a roulette table. I don't usually go to casinos, but the dream was very clear. In the dream I placed a ten pound note on the number nine, the wheel was spun and the dice miraculously landed on the number nine. Within a couple of days of having the dream, I found myself at a casino with two friends. Remembering and trusting the dream, I chose to play a couple of goes at the roulette. The first was to understand how it worked! On the second, I chose the number nine and I was probably the least surprised person in the room when the ball landed on the number nine! It was exactly what I had been *expecting*!

I went on to play a few rounds of Black Jack and on each round I was a winner. I have no doubt that this was because I was on what they call a 'winning streak'. I was feeling lucky. My thoughts were aligned with being a winner. It was the last time I will ever visit a casino, as I haven't had any such dreams since.

Let me be clear about one thing, though: gambling is definitely *not* one of the recommended ways to become a Money Magnet! However, if you receive a powerful intuition to do something, then I strongly recommend you follow it. Practise recognizing the 'knowing' voice in you (as opposed to the fearful, anxious voice in you).

The more you start to trust yourself and the power of your thoughts, the more freedom you will have to create the life and fortune that you wish to create.

The thought to trust is normally the very first thought that you experience. It's the one that comes before all the excuses and reasons why you can't do what you want to do. This is brilliantly illustrated in the following story, summarized from the book *Leadership and Self-Deception* by the Arbinger Institute.

A father is awoken at 4 a.m. by his baby crying in another room. His wife is still sleeping peacefully at his side. His first thought is to get up and see to the baby. However, this is swiftly followed by a second thought: 'Yes, but it's nice and warm in this bed and I don't want to get up right now.' His third thought is likely to be about his wife: 'How come she wasn't woken by our baby crying?' The fourth thought is, 'I have a long day at work ahead of me. It's not fair that I have to get up now to see to the child when that's her job!' His fifth thought is that his wife is clearly not a good mother!

Can you see what is happening? Can you see how we can talk ourselves out of doing the right thing? Even worse, can you see how your thoughts can create whole scenarios and meanings from nothing when you allow them to? And how often do you end up blaming or judging someone else instead of taking responsibility for not listening and responding to your initial gut instinct?

If, for example, your mind is telling you to go and get a job, or write a book, or sort out a debt repayment plan, it is time to start paying attention! It is far more exhausting to resist what your mind really wants to do, and you'll find that life is a lot more fun when you just get on and do what you know needs to be done!

Value Your Time

Each of us has the same amount of time in a day. The difference is in how we choose to spend it. It is the decisions you make every day, and how you choose to spend your time, that value who you are as a person.

> *'Time is really the only capital that any human being has, and the only thing he can't afford to lose.'*
> – **Thomas Edison**

I love spending time with people. In the past, if someone invited me to meet up with them, my knee jerk response would always be to go. Then I realized that my book wasn't getting written, I was behind with my accounts and my business plan had big holes in it; worst of all, I hadn't had time for a holiday for months! I realized that I had a limiting belief that I'd repeated often enough for it to have become a mantra: 'There are never enough hours in the day.' That is a mantra of scarcity.

When I realized what I was doing, I knew to change it to a more empowering mantra: 'Everything that matters will get done.' When I got clear on my goals, and what I really wanted, it was easy to plan my time to fit in everything that was important. I started to say 'no' more to things that didn't feel 100% right, or which weren't aligned with my goals. I started to manage my time better so I could do more.

When you are in your flow, you think nothing of waking up an hour or two earlier to write the book, or of staying up late to coach someone in another country. You are lit up by your life. You love what you do, and so you will look at cramming every minute of your day with more of it. When you really want more, you will find a way to have more time in your day. If you don't value your time, you can bet that no one else will value your time. Resolve now to account for every hour of your day, and to enjoy a rich and fulfilled life!

Value Your Money

People who value the money they have, attract more of it. If you spend your money as quickly as you get it, you are not valuing it. Demonstrate how much you value your money by knowing how much you have on any given day, and how you are investing your time and resources to make you more money.

On the one hand, look for ways to save money. On the other hand, look for ways to create more money coming in. It's an easy equation: to have more money in your bank account than you have now, you need to earn more than you spend, and to know whether you are overspending, you need to measure and track your money as a regular habit. Start getting interested in your balance sheets! Complete the exercises in this book.

Value Your Skills and Abilities

What is your gift to the world? What comes naturally to you that might be difficult for others? For example, my friend Claire is fantastic at detailed work and doing her accounts, but she hates public speaking. I love to address a crowd of people but I'm not too keen on doing my accounts. Recognizing where your strengths and natural talents lie is key to accessing your wealth.

So Claire uses her attention to detail on a money-making website she's created, and I use my people skills to make money through speaking and collaborative ventures. The interesting thing is that when we know how to do something naturally, it is easy not to acknowledge its value. Claire might think that everyone can do detailed work, and be oblivious to the huge value she provides for others.

I didn't value my natural oratory skills until there was a neighbourhood meeting to protest against council plans to erect a mobile mast in our area. The three 'leaders' at the front of the room had no leadership skills, and lacked the powerful voice needed to enlist support and action from the rest of the people in the room. It was then that I realized my value.

> *'Everybody is a genius. But if you judge a fish by its ability to climb a tree, it will live its whole life believing that it is stupid.'*
>
> – **Albert Einstein**

■ *Case Study: Honour Your Authentic Value*

Filipe de Moura has a gift for, and a real love of, singing opera. At a group event, I remember asking Filipe if he would sing for us, there and then. Filipe considered the request and responded calmly with a 'no'. He explained that to offer his voice in song was for him a real gift. It came from a place of total passion and real love, where he committed his heart and soul. He wasn't prepared to deliver such a performance there and then. In that moment, Filipe established his value. We now yearned to hear him sing all the more. In fact, it wasn't until a year later, when I invited him onto my TV show as a guest, that I finally heard Filipe perform. He stole the show and moved us all to tears. You can find out more about Filipe at www.filipedemoura.com

Don't give away your gift too freely if you want others to value it.

<u>Money Magnet Mindset Tool: Acknowledging Your Skills and Abilities</u>

Note down now your strengths and your skills and what you love to do (there is normally a correlation between the two). Ask your friends if you are not sure:

....

....

....

Value Your Environment

What do your home and office say about you? Is your home the home of someone who values themselves? Is it a place where you are happy to invite guests? Do you love your home?

> *Your home is the outer reflection of the inner you.*

If there is anything you don't love about your home, now is the time to do something about it. It costs nothing to clear your clutter, or to clean some cupboards. Imagine that the Queen (or an equivalent person) was coming to visit. What changes would you make before their arrival? Are you not worth valuing in the same way?

If you cannot currently change your home to how you'd ideally like it, choose to love it as it is. Accept what you want to change, make a plan to effect the changes and then embrace it as it is. Gratitude for what you currently have (some people don't have a home) will attract more things for which you can be grateful. So, rather than moan about what you don't have, celebrate what you do have!

The main guidelines for loving your environment are as follows:

- Keep it clear of clutter.

- Make good use of colour and lighting.

- Use natural plants.

- Repair any non-working appliances.

- Clean and redecorate regularly.

- Use eco-friendly paints and appliances.

- Invest in as good a bed as you can afford.

- Keep TVs out of the bedroom.

- Work as a team to keep it looking good.

- Entertain guests in your home.

Value Your Work

I remember falling in love and thinking that I wanted to provide everything I could for the man I loved. I was inspired to create more value from my business so we could create an amazing life together. It was then that I questioned why I wouldn't want to create an amazing life for *myself*.

If you are not motivated by your work, or you are always complaining about having to work too hard, you might want to change something. You will either want to change your *job* if it feels like too much hard work, or you will want to change your *mind* about it being hard work. How about choosing to 'work smart' instead? Look to see how you can give as much value as you can. Remember, the more you give the more you receive, and the universe works in mysterious ways!

> *'Choose a job you love and you will never have to work a day in your life.'*
> **– Confucius**

If you have a nagging doubt in the back of your mind that you don't like what you are doing for work, it is better to face up to it than to ignore it and put on a brave (but secretly complaining) face. As long as you are unhappy, you will find it impossible to value what you do, and to attract more value into your life. When you look yourself in the eye and ask whether you love what you do or not, you will find out whether you really *don't* like it, or whether you are just complaining as an excuse not to give 100% to it. Once you have that clarity, you can then take the appropriate action.

Whatever you do, don't settle for anything less than what you want for yourself.

Value Your Friends

> *'You are the average of the five people you spend the most time with.'*
> **– Jim Rohn**

It might seem a really obvious thing to suggest that you love your friends. After all, why would they be your friends if you didn't love them? Well, one of the reasons why you may be surrounded by friends that you no longer like or respect is because you don't know how to say 'no' or 'goodbye' to them. If you fear being rejected, you may find the idea of rejecting someone else too uncomfortable. You may fear having to face life alone. If you are spending time with people who don't make you feel good and don't support your values and goals, it is time to move on. They will get over it. There are 7 billion people on the planet. They will find a new friend; you will find a new friend.

Maybe you have life-long friends who dip in and out of your life. Have you noticed that they always appear at the perfect moment? Synchronicities like this reaffirm how we attract energetic mirrors of ourselves. If you don't like what you see in the mirror you can either change the friend or change yourself. Personally, I advocate that you take responsibility for who shows up in your life, and stay focused on their good qualities rather than being judgemental about their failings. Accept it if a friend chooses to move away, as it may be that you are clearing space for a new friend to match your new Money Magnet vibration.

Take a moment to look at the five people who feature most in your daily life. Write down what you love about them and the things that also drive you mad about them!

....

....

....

....

....

Now recognize these qualities in yourself, both the good and the bad.

Valuing yourself means valuing every part of you, including the parts that you'd rather ignore. Your friends are there to help you accept all the parts of yourself. Love your friends wholly and unconditionally.

Chapter 10

Believe You Can Do It!

*'The strongest single factor in acquiring abundance
is self-esteem: believing you can do it, believing
you deserve it, believing you will get it.'*
– **Jerry Gillies**

I asked Andrew Sage, the designer whose story we looked at in Chapter 7, what message he would share with someone who might be feeling overwhelmed and impoverished, but who has the root of an idea on which to focus. He offered three pointers:

1. Don't give up.

2. Be yourself and trust yourself.

3. Know that you can do anything.

There are plenty of people out there who will tell you that you can't do it. The trick is to mix with those who tell you that you *can* do it. Take time out to go to events where you will mingle with like-minded, 'can do', entrepreneurial people. Join the networks of people who believe in supporting the dreams of others. You can have your own business without having to do it all alone. Help others to fulfil their dreams and aspirations, and allow yourself to be supported by others. It doesn't need to be hard work. Look for people who have already trodden the path that you want to tread. Find yourself a mentor who inspires you. When you find yourself the right person, don't hesitate to ask them for their support.

When you find the right course or programme, act on your instincts and invest in yourself. The difference between the people who make the money and those who read all the books, attend all the seminars and use up all their savings, is that those who make it work are those who take action outside their comfort zone. As John Wayne was quoted as saying, 'Courage is being scared to death and saddling up anyway.'

'Anyone can give up, it's the easiest thing in the world to do. But to hold it together when everyone else would understand if you fell apart, that's true strength.'
– **Anon**

The trick is to *commit* to what you want. Be someone who honours their word, and when you commit to yourself that you are going to do something, you know that it will be done. Your word becomes your gospel and your truth. That is where you will find your self-belief.

Clear up anything that is incomplete – where you've said you'll do something and you haven't done it. Either get it done, or communicate to the relevant person that it won't be done. In doing so you will immediately enhance how you perceive yourself. Self-belief is an inside job. Nobody else can do it for you. Only you know if you are someone who honours their own word, and who does what they say they are going to do.

Feedback and Forgiveness

If you haven't always done things the right way in the past, or if you feel that you've only failed up until this point, can you forgive yourself? Can you accept that failure is only when you do nothing at all – and even then it may just be that you needed some space to take a step back and look at things from a new perspective.

Most millionaires failed time and time again before they became an 'overnight success'. Embrace your failures as opportunities to receive valuable feedback. Embrace another's failure as an opportunity to look at how you can be responsible. For example, I used to complain that my PA hadn't done something as I'd wanted it done. When I stopped judging and making it about her, and instead looked to see how I could be more responsible, I realized that I hadn't really trusted her to get it right in the first place and my communication hadn't been clear. As soon as I delivered clearer instructions, the job was done perfectly, and I learnt to trust her with more and more stuff.

Don't Let Anyone Tell You Otherwise

Leaders find new ways of thinking and embrace new ways of doing things. Most people resist change, and are not keen on new things until they are proven. Once you have found your passion, don't allow anyone to dim your flame.

Don't let yourself be swayed by others. And don't allow the resigned voice within you to rule your life. You are worth so much more than that. You have a wealth of abundance waiting to spring forth. Your job is to keep the tap turned on by maintaining a positive, 'can do' mindset.

> *'Promise me you'll always remember: you are braver than you believe, and stronger than you seem, and smarter than you think.'*
> – **Christopher Robin to Pooh**

Maintain a Money Magnet Mindset

We all experience moments when we believe we can accomplish anything. Next time you feel full of possibility, capture the moment:

- How are you standing or sitting?

- Is your head up or down?

- How does your body feel?

- If you were to recapture your exact position and posture, what would you need to write down?

- What happened just before you felt like this?

- What, in particular, triggered these feelings of 'Wow, I can do anything!'?

Note it all down. You might want to start a collection of 'wow moments' in your life. After all, most of us waste far too much energy looking down at what doesn't work, and not enough time on the empowering, happy, 'I can do anything' moments.

When was the last time you had a big smile on your face, or experienced a fit of the giggles or a belly laugh? Can you remember how it felt? If I asked you to recreate it right now, can you feel where the giggle starts in your body? Can you feel the outer edges of your mouth start to curl upwards and your eyes feel brighter?

You can do anything if you believe you can. It all starts in the mind. The mind is connected to the body. Start paying attention to your body so you can practise recreating those moments full of self-belief.

Affirmations

> *'Whether you think you can, or you think you can't –*
> *you're right.'*
>
> – **Henry Ford**

If you have a natural tendency to think the worst, you need to retrain your mind to think of only the best possible outcomes, and to embrace only the best aspects of yourself. Look at what you could say to yourself that would reinforce your own self-belief. You are already talking to yourself all the time. We just want to make sure that your voice is that of a positive, supportive friend, rather than a discouraging enemy.

Affirmations are short, positive, and personal statements which, repeated often enough, can become beliefs. You can create your own empowering affirmations by using the following guidelines:

- Make them personal, i.e. start with 'I'.

- Use the present tense.

- Keep them short and powerful.

- Exclude any negative commands, i.e. 'not' or 'no'.

- Ideally, employ a natural rhythm or rhyme.

- Ensure they make you feel good when you say them.

Here are some examples of empowering affirmations:

- 'I am a Money Magnet.'

- 'I love who I am just as I am.'

- 'I make a difference every day.'

- 'I love my life!'

- 'Money follows me wherever I go.'

- 'I attract money easily.'

- 'It's easy to earn money.'

- 'I love finding ways to have more money.'

- 'I love opening my bills/paying my taxes.'

- 'I love money and money loves me.'

- 'I am worth millions.'

- 'I believe in miracles.'

- 'I am in love.'

- 'I'm in the money!'

Money Magnet Mindset Tool: Creating Your Own Affirmations

Now write down some affirmations of your own and put them in places where you will see them frequently throughout the day. This is about reinforcing this new belief into your unconscious mind.

Peak Performance coach Joseph McClendan III recommends that you use a mini trampoline and bounce on it each morning while listening to the same favourite track of music and saying your affirmations out loud. It sounds a bit crazy, but it is highly effective. My favourite track for this exercise is 'Higher Love' by Stevie Winwood.

McClendan also suggests that you paint a picture of what you want and visualize it while bouncing on the trampoline. The resonance of bouncing helps to ground the new beliefs and vision into your body in a way that allows you to easily accept them. Don't knock it until you've tried it! If it feels strange, then consider it great practice for pushing through your comfort zone and daring to do something that others would ridicule. It is in these actions that you practise becoming a leader and a Money Magnet!

Practise Saying 'Yes!'

Say 'yes' more often. One of my clients realized that she peppered her conversations with the word 'no', even when she meant 'yes'. Once she became aware of what she was doing, she was able to consciously correct herself and she felt so much clearer and more powerful when she started using the word 'yes'. She was finally giving up her resistance to having the life she wanted.

Paying attention to your language is quite possibly the most effective way of influencing your mind and your self-belief. Watch out for the times when you may be blaming factors outside yourself, and in so doing, making yourself a victim. That has no power in it.

Money Magnet Mindset Tool: Changing Your Language

If you are angry with someone, or you are feeling poor and fed up with life, avoid saying, 'I am angry' or 'I am feeling poor and fed up with life.' Instead, add the words 'a part of me', so that it becomes, 'A part of me is feeling angry', or 'A part of me is feeling poor and fed up with life.'

That way you leave the door of possibility open for the rest of you!

Try it and you will be amazed at how empowering it feels!

Look at what else you are saying unconsciously. Work with a friend or a coach who can pull you up on anything you are saying that does not support what you want in life. Create an agreement that they have permission to correct you at any time. The first step is to become aware of your language, and then to change it.

How Can I?

The disempowering statements around money that I hear the most are: 'I can't' and 'I can't afford it.' As soon as the words 'I can't' are uttered, you are effectively cutting off all possibilities. The phrase has become an accepted alternative to saying 'no', because people are less comfortable saying 'no'.

For example, a friend of mine recently announced to me on the way to a night out that she couldn't afford to buy any drinks. I asked her to be more powerful in her choice of words. She responded by saying that she chose not to spend her money on alcoholic drinks, and would be choosing to drink water instead during the evening. That was her choice, and can you see how much more powerful that is as a statement of what she valued?

Most of the time, 'I can't afford it' simply means 'I would rather spend my money on something else.' If you are trying to sell something to somebody and they tell you that they can't afford it, it means that you haven't demonstrated enough value to them. We spend our money according to what we value. A much better approach would be to switch the words around into the question: 'How could I afford it?' By just asking this question, you will start to see new opportunities and ideas open up for you.

Visualize the Outcome

Always focus on the outcome. Visualize the outcome that you want. Your imagination is so powerful and your unconscious mind doesn't recognize the difference between imagination and reality. This is why world-class athletes employ visualization techniques in their preparation to win medals. They visualize every detail of the race and it going according to plan, right up until they are standing on the podium holding the gold medal.

> *An entrepreneur is someone who has a vision of what could happen and who makes it happen by visualizing how it could happen.*

You too can use visualization in your daily life. If you are planning to make a number of phone calls, for example, you can visualize a positive outcome from each of them.

Claudia was struggling to pick up the phone to make her sales calls. She was worrying about saying the right thing and coming across as a pushy salesperson. I encouraged her to visualize having a gorgeous conversation with each person in a way that was easy for her to make a sale. Claudia's energy then shifted to being excited and full of anticipation, and she started to achieve the sales results she wanted.

Now if Claudia had simply visualized the outcome without ever picking up the phone, there would be a limit to how much she could achieve! In the same way that an athlete needs to train for the race as well as visualize the desired outcome, I recommend that you use visualization as a tool in your toolbox, rather than the 'be-all and end-all'.

> *'You are living simultaneously in two worlds, two realities:*
> *the inner reality of your thoughts, emotions and attitudes,*
> *and the outer reality of people, places, things and events.*
> *Because we fail to separate these Inner and Outer worlds,*
> *we allow ourselves to become dominated by the Outer*
> *world of appearances, and we use the Inner world solely as*
> *a "mirror" for whatever happens to us.*
>
> *'Our Inner world reacts constantly, and because we spend*
> *all of our time simply reacting, we never experience our*
> *power. Ironically, you begin changing your reality the day,*
> *the hour, the minute you cease constantly reacting to it.'*
>
> **– John Kehoe**

Training yourself to have a Money Magnet Mindset is about learning to manage your automatic emotional responses when you perceive that you don't have enough money. When you can give up being a victim of circumstances and choose to take responsibility for how you think and talk about your money and your life, you can start to create the money and the life you want.

Imagine that your day starts with getting a big bill in the post. Most people would succumb to thoughts like, 'Oh no! What a bad start to the day', and guess what, things would start to degenerate from that point on! If you can master your thoughts so you respond to a bill as something that just needs to be paid, you can then simply take the actions to pay it, or, if need be, to find the monies to pay it, without any drama or emotion. You become the master of your money and your life.

Be Grateful

The mindset of gratitude brings you more things for which you can be grateful. Make it a habit at certain times each day to stop and take a moment to be grateful. You might even wish to set an alarm on your phone to make sure you take the time out to train your brain. We learn so many habits in life, so now is the time to review your habits and decide if they are working for you or against you.

MONEY MAGNET MINDSET HABITS – A DAILY COMMITMENT TO BECOMING A MONEY MAGNET

- Start the day by visualizing how it will turn out perfectly.

- Declare out loud an affirmation for the day, or sing it in the shower!

- Keep affirmation reminders in places around your home, car and office.

- Listen to personal development CDs in the car and while travelling.

- Read an uplifting book last thing at night.

- Be vigilant about what you watch on TV.

- Be unstoppable in pursuit of your goals.

- Train yourself to be more positive in your language.

- Give yourself a break when things don't go according to plan.

- When you are doing one thing, focus 100% on that one thing.

- Keep a gratitude journal to capture the wealth in your life.

Afterword

'Aerodynamically, the bumblebee shouldn't be
able to fly, but the bumblebee doesn't know
that, so it goes on flying anyway.'
– Mary Kay Ash

Anything is possible if you believe it is. Businesses start from an idea – just as a seed grows into a sapling and then into a tree. Brad Burton went from £25,000 of debt to owning a business worth millions. He had an idea to have 200 networking groups in the UK. In less than six years, his business 4Networking counted over 300 groups, and Brad shares his 'can do' message as a speaker as widely as possible to inspire others. When asked what religion he follows, Brad replied, *'Braddism: hurt few, help many, live life!'*

The world is changing. The days of greed and abuse of power are fading. Governments, politicians, and company executives are being held to account. It would be easy to make money the bad boy, and I have seen many people reject money in the belief that having it makes you a bad person. It is not money that is the culprit, but the behaviour of people who seek to have money over and above all else – including love and respect for their fellow human beings.

Today, we live in a world where we embrace entrepreneurship and the possibility that anyone can create their own business. The future is one of creativity and possibility and love, and small businesses are sprouting daily.

All you need to do is find out what inspires you over and above the money, and then allow it to pull you forward in a way that is hard to resist. Find the vision that you have for yourself, and the world that lights you up and makes you jump out of bed each morning.

Find out why you were put on this Earth.

Find Your Big Vision

I remember attending a marketing workshop run by Rachel Elnaugh, former star of *Dragons' Den* and founder of Red Letter Days. When Rachel asked us for our big reason why we wanted success, I started to say that I wanted to be a bestselling author and speaker, touring the world to inspire as many people as possible. That's what I had been saying for a few years.

But Rachel invited me to go deeper within, and to look for something that really moved me. I remembered reading the book *Half the Sky,* and in that moment I felt quite overwhelmed by something that was far larger than me. I picked up my pen and found myself writing down the biggest vision for my life I'd ever had. It was to be someone who made a real difference to solving global poverty in the way that William Wilberforce had done for the abolition of slavery. The vision was so huge that it both lit me up and terrified me – did you know that fear and excitement are physically the same chemical reaction?

Recommended Resources

Books

A Return to Love, Marianne Williamson (HarperPerennial, 1993)

The Art of Possibility, Rosamund Stone Zander & Benjamin Zander (HBS Press, 2000)

Ask and It Is Given, Esther and Jerry Hicks (Hay House, 2008)

The Blue Sweater, Jacqueline Novogratz (Rodale Press, 2010)

Choices, Dr Shad Helmstetter (Pocket, 1990)

Eat That Frog, Brian Tracy (Mobius, 2004)

The Field, Lynne McTaggart (Element, 2003)

Flirt Coach, Peta Heskell (Thorsons, 2009)

From Stress to Success in Just 31 Days, Dr John F. Demartini (Hay House, 2009)

Fulfilled, Deirdre Bounds (Pearson Life, 2009)

Get Off Your Arse, Brad Burton (4Publishing, 2009)

Half The Sky, Nicholas D. Kristoff and Sheryl Wudunn (Virago, 2010)

Hope for the Flowers, Trina Paulus (Paulist Press, revised 2000)

Just Get On With It, Ali Campbell (Hay House, 2010)

The Law of Attraction, Esther and Jerry Hicks (Hay House, 2007)

Leadership and Self Deception, The Arbinger Institute (Penguin, 2007)

Miracles Happen, Mary Kay Ash (Quill, 2003)

The Quantum Warrior, John Kehoe (Zoetic Inc., 2011)

Rich Dad Poor Dad, Robert Kiyosaki (Plata Publishing, 2011)

The Richest Man in Babylon, George S. Clason (Media Eight International Publishing Limited, 2012)

The Road Less Travelled, M. Scott Peck, (Simon & Schuster, 1978)

The Rules of Wealth, Richard Templar (Prentice Hall, 2006)

Secrets of the Millionaire Mind, T. Harv Eker (Piatkus, 2005)

Secrets of the Wealth Accelerators, Paul Avins (Paul Avins Enterprises Ltd., 2011)

Sheconomics, Karen J. Pine and Simonne Gnessen, (Headline, 2009)

The Slight Edge, Jeff Olson (Success Books, 2011)

Think and Grow Rich, Napoleon Hill (Vermilion, 2004)

What You See is What You Get, Alan Sugar (Pan, 2011)

You Can Have What You Want, Michael Neill (Hay House, 2009)

Audio, DVD and online resources

What the Bleep Do We Know? DVD (Revolver Entertainment, 2005)

The Art of Exceptional Living, Jim Rohn, Audiobook (Nightingale-Conant, 2003; Model: JR940-006)

Visit Jerry Gilles's Moneylove blog at http://moneyloveblog.com/

Find out more about Brad Burton's unique look at life at www.bradburton.biz

JOIN THE HAY HOUSE FAMILY

As the leading self-help, mind, body and spirit publisher in the UK, we'd like to welcome you to our family so that you can enjoy all the benefits our website has to offer.

 EXTRACTS from a selection of your favourite author titles

 COMPETITIONS, PRIZES & SPECIAL OFFERS Win extracts, money off, downloads and so much more

 LISTEN to a range of radio interviews and our latest audio publications

 CELEBRATE YOUR BIRTHDAY An inspiring gift will be sent your way

 LATEST NEWS Keep up with the latest news from and about our authors

 ATTEND OUR AUTHOR EVENTS Be the first to hear about our author events

iPHONE APPS Download your favourite app for your iPhone

 HAY HOUSE INFORMATION Ask us anything, all enquiries answered

join us online at **www.hayhouse.co.uk**

 292B Kensal Road, London W10 5BE
T: 020 8962 1230 E: info@hayhouse.co.uk

ABOUT THE AUTHOR

Marie-Claire Carlyle has spent most of her working life coaching others to fulfill their true potential. As sales manager and later as sales director, Marie-Claire used her skills and knowledge to ensure that her team consistently overachieved sales targets. As a professional coach and feng shui consultant, Marie-Claire helps her clients to clear out the clutter that hides their true magnificence and wealth.

Having discovered the way to wealth herself, Marie-Claire developed the 'How to Become a Money Magnet' one-day workshop. The results were consistently positive and she was asked to capture the essence of the workshop in a book, *How to Become a Money Magnet*.

Marie-Claire runs her own coaching and consultancy business, helping both companies and individuals to achieve their true potential, in every sense of the word. As well as writing several books, Marie-Claire founded Miracle Club which provides affordable group coaching to inspire everyone to fulfill their true potential for happiness (www.miracleclub.com).

Marie-Claire holds two business degrees, and is a qualified life coach (DipLCH) and NLP practitioner, and an accredited feng shui consultant (FSSA) and Space Clearer. Marie-Claire also studied at the College of Psychic Studies, The School of Insight and Intuition and extensively with Diana Cooper, where she qualified as a Transform Your Life teacher. She has taught at local colleges, where her subjects included life coaching, cosmic ordering and feng shui, and she now facilitates workshops and events across the world.

www.marieclairecarlyle.com